OECD PROCEEDINGS

GLOBALISATION AND THE ENVIRONMENT

Perspectives from OECD and Dynamic Non-Member Economies

PUBLISHER'S NOTE

The following texts are published in their original form to permit faster distribution at a lower cost.
The views expressed are those of the authors,
and do not necessarily reflect those of the Organisation or of its Member countries.

ORGANISATION FOR ECONOMIC CO-OPERATION AND DEVELOPMENT

ORGANISATION FOR ECONOMIC CO-OPERATION AND DEVELOPMENT

Pursuant to Article 1 of the Convention signed in Paris on 14th December 1960, and which came into force on 30th September 1961, the Organisation for Economic Co-operation and Development (OECD) shall promote policies designed:

- to achieve the highest sustainable economic growth and employment and a rising standard of living in Member countries, while maintaining financial stability, and thus to contribute to the development of the world economy;
- to contribute to sound economic expansion in Member as well as non-member countries in the process of economic development; and
- to contribute to the expansion of world trade on a multilateral, non-discriminatory basis in accordance with international obligations.

The original Member countries of the OECD are Austria, Belgium, Canada, Denmark, France, Germany, Greece, Iceland, Ireland, Italy, Luxembourg, the Netherlands, Norway, Portugal, Spain, Sweden, Switzerland, Turkey, the United Kingdom and the United States. The following countries became Members subsequently through accession at the dates indicated hereafter: Japan (28th April 1964), Finland (28th January 1969), Australia (7th June 1971), New Zealand (29th May 1973), Mexico (18th May 1994), the Czech Republic (21st December 1995), Hungary (7th May 1996), Poland (22nd November 1996) and the Republic of Korea (12th December 1996). The Commission of the European Communities takes part in the work of the OECD (Article 13 of the OECD Convention).

FOREWORD

Globalisation is likely to pose important challenges to, and opportunities for, environmental policy. For example, in the absence of a sound domestic environmental policy framework, globalisation could intensify existing, and create new, pressures on the environment and natural resources through intensified trade and investment. On the other hand, globalisation could promote a more efficient allocation of environmental factors of production and use, as well as wider diffusion of cleaner technologies. Governments are now confronting the challenge of how to optimise the environmental and other benefits of globalisation.

Business and industry are at the heart of globalisation. More intense competition, the world-wide organisation of production and distribution systems and services, and rapid technological change are some of the principal drivers of global business strategies. The manner in which environmental and economic policies stimulate business behaviour will help shape the environmental consequences of globalisation.

To better understand the key policy issues associated with the globalisation and environment relationship, in November 1997 the OECD organised a workshop on the theme of "Globalisation and the Environment: New Challenges for the Public and Private Sectors". The workshop was held within the framework of the OECD's Policy Dialogue with the Dynamic Non-Member Economies[1] and brought together more than 80 policy-makers, business persons and academics from OECD Member countries and non-member economies in Asia and Latin America. Professor Emil Salim, Centre for Policy and Implementation Studies, Indonesia and Mr. Bjorn Stigson, President, World Business Council for Sustainable Development, Switzerland co-chaired the workshop.

This volume presents selected papers from the workshop. The views expressed are those of the respective authors and do not necessarily reflect the views of the OECD, its Member countries or of the institutions to which the authors are affiliated. The volume was edited by Mr. Chris Chung, OECD Environment Directorate. It is published on the responsibility of the Secretary-General of the OECD.

---

[1] Currently the Dynamic Non-Member Economies are: Argentina, Brazil, Chile, Chinese Taipei, Hong Kong (China), Malaysia, the Philippines, Singapore and Thailand. Experts from China, India and Indonesia participate in selected events.

TABLE OF CONTENTS

GLOBALISATION AND THE ENVIRONMENT: NEW CHALLENGES FOR THE PUBLIC AND PRIVATE SECTORS

Chris Chung and Brendan Gillespie
Environment Directorate, OECD

1.0   Introduction

It is generally agreed that economic activity is becoming more "globalised". There is less agreement, however, about what this will mean for individuals. Optimists stress increased levels of economic output, income and employment, while pessimists emphasise increasing inequalities within and between societies and an increasing potential for social tension.

Economic globalisation has been defined as "a process in which the structures of economic markets, technologies and communication patterns become progressively more international over time" (page 7)[1]. Higher levels of investment, deeper liberalisation of international trade regimes, intensified competition and rapid technological change are some of the main drivers of this process. They can impact on the environment in a variety of ways. However, it is clear that a more global, competitive business sector, as well as effective public policy frameworks, will play central roles in mediating the economy-environment relationship. As ever, the policy challenge is to find ways to maximise the benefits and minimise the costs.

It was within this broad context that, in November 1997, the OECD held a workshop on "Globalisation and the Environment: New Challenges for the Public and Private Sectors", involving policy-makers, business persons and academics from OECD Member countries, Asia and Latin America. The workshop was the third to be held on environment policy issues under the auspices of the OECD's Policy Dialogue with the Dynamic Non-Member Economies (DNMEs)[2].

The objectives of the workshop were:

- to discuss the environmental challenges and opportunities for OECD Member countries and the DNMEs, and for government and business, arising from the globalisation of the world economy;

---

[1]   OECD, 1997a: *Economic Globalisation and the Environment*. OECD. Paris.

[2]   The proceedings of the two previous workshops have been published as OECD, 1994: *Applying Economic Instruments to Environmental Policies in OECD and Dynamic Non-Member Economies*; and OECD, 1997: *Cleaner Production and Waste Minimisation in OECD and Dynamic Non-Member Economies*. OECD. Paris.

- to review the strategies being developed by the public and private sectors in response to these challenges and opportunities, with particular reference to trade, investment, technology and environmental management; and

- to identify areas where shared analysis of the globalisation and environment relationship could strengthen dialogue and co-operation between the DNMEs and OECD Member countries.

This paper introduces the key environmental challenges to, and opportunities for, the public and private sectors in responding to the process of economic globalisation. Its purpose is to provide a framework within which to situate the papers in the remainder of the volume.

2.0   Globalisation and the Environment: Context

The context in which policies for sustainable development are designed and implemented is being transformed by the process of globalisation. The environmental impacts of globalisation relate to the scale effects of increased output, the structural effects of shifts in the types and location of economic activities, the technology effects of utilising different technologies and product effects from the production and consumption of new product mixes[3].

Globalisation can promote a more efficient and less-environmentally damaging pattern of economic development by shifting production from raw materials-based manufacturing to knowledge-based service industries; promoting the wider diffusion and adoption of cleaner technologies; alleviating poverty and its associated adverse environmental effects; and generating the additional wealth necessary to finance environmental investments. In these ways, globalisation could help uncouple economic growth from pollution generation and resource consumption, and, thereby, foster sustainable development[4].

However, countervailing forces could offset the realisation of this potential. Increased economic activity could result in overall resource consumption and pollution trends rising, despite lower levels per unit of output. Furthermore, even if the environmental and welfare effects of globalisation were positive globally, the distribution of environmental pressures would differ, depending on comparative advantages in assimilative capacity and resource endowments. In addition, there will be "winners" and "losers" within and between countries, raising issues of equity and social justice. In this context, questions have been raised about the distributional implications of increased consumption patterns and the share of world resources consumed by different groups of countries.

OECD analysis shows that the non-OECD share of world GDP could increase from about 40 per cent in 1995 to more than 60 per cent by 2020, and its share in world trade could rise from one-third to one-half. Living standards could show a more dramatic shift: in the non-OECD area they could rise by 270 per cent while in the OECD area this figure might be 80 per cent[5]. In this scenario, OECD

---

[3]   OECD, 1997a: See Footnote 1.

[4]   OECD, 1997b: *The World in 2020. Towards a New Global Age.* OECD. Paris.

[5]   OECD, 1997b: See Footnote 4.

economic performance and key environmental trends would be strongly influenced by the policies and performance of the DNMEs, especially in countries such as Brazil, China, India and Indonesia.

As the table below shows, eight countries -- the E8 -- will have an increasingly important role in shaping future global environmental trends: Brazil, China, Germany, India, Indonesia, Japan, Russia and the US. The industrial countries of this group shape global trends through their economic strength, their high levels of consumption, and their dominance of technology. The influence of the other countries of the E8 stems mainly from their large populations, their rapid economic development, and their rich biodiversity. Together, these eight countries account for 56 per cent of the world's population, 59 per cent of its economic output, 58 per cent of its carbon emissions, and 53 per cent of its forests[6].

Eight Environmentally Important Countries

Country	Share of World Population % 1996	Share of Gross World Product % 1994	Share of World Carbon Emissions % 1995	Share of World Forest Area % 1990	Share of World Flowering Plant Species % 1990 [a]
United States	5	26	23	6	8
Russian Federation	3	2	7	21	9
Japan	2	17	5	0.7	2
Germany	1	8	4	0.3	1
China	21	2	13	4	12
India	17	1	4	2	6
Indonesia	4	0.7	1	3	8
Brazil	3	2	1	16	22
TOTAL	56	59	58	53	..

Note:

a) Based on a total of 250 000 known species. Total could not be calculated due to overlap in species among countries.

Source: Flavin, C., 1997: "The Legacy of Rio" in *State of the World 1997*. Worldwatch Institute/ W.W. Norton and Co. New York.

In June 1997, the UN General Assembly Special Session (UNGASS) reviewed progress made in the five years since the Rio "Earth Summit". The overall assessment was that, despite positive developments in some areas, progress has been disappointing. The state of the environment has continued to worsen in respect of a variety of indicators[7]. In the coming decades, environmental pressures will be intensified through such problems as the increasing consumption of fossil fuels, rising volumes of hazardous and other wastes, the concentration of populations in 'megacities' and a more intensive exploitation of natural resources such as forests, fisheries and freshwater.

---

[6] Flavin, C., 1997: "The Legacy of Rio" in *State of the World 1997*. Worldwatch Institute/W.W. Norton and Co. New York.

[7] See generally UNEP, 1997: *Global Environmental Outlook 1. Global State of the Environment Report 1997*. Oxford University Press. New York.

Solid achievements will need to be shown by the time of the "Rio+10" conference in 2002 if political and public momentum in support of the sustainable development agenda is to be maintained and enhanced. It will be crucial to have strengthened the dialogue among, and commitments by, all stakeholders so that they are prepared to take the actions necessary to implement sustainable development policies. In this context, building the necessary consensus will require, *inter alia*, improved "bottom-up" mechanisms that promote wide consultation and open exchange of views.

As we approach the twenty-first century, a key policy issue is: will globalisation help efforts to promote sustainable development, or will it make the task more difficult? For example, how will globalisation change the distribution of environmental pressures -- and associated responsibilities -- among countries? How will patterns of production and consumption be affected?

Relevant Papers in this Volume

♦ Tom Jones: "Economic Globalisation and the Environment: An Overview of the Linkages" (page 17).

♦ Derek Osborn: "Beyond UNGASS: Challenges for OECD and Dynamic Non-Member Economies" (page 29).

♦ Eduardo Viola: "Globalisation, Environmentalism and New Transnational Social Forces" (page 39).

♦ Djamester Simarmata: "Free Trade and the Global Environment as International Public Goods" (page 53).

3.0   Business Responses to the Environmental Challenges and Opportunities of Globalisation

The manner in which environmental and economic policies affect business behaviour will have an important influence on the environmental strategies adopted by business. Despite some progress achieved in implementing "win-win" approaches such as eco-efficiency, cleaner production and waste minimisation, the challenge facing most companies is how to meet medium- or long-term environmental goals where trade-offs are required with the company's short-term financial performance.

Profit maximisation is the crucial factor in business strategies in all types of companies, and the intensification of competition associated with globalisation will put further pressure on profit margins. On the other hand, some major multinational companies recognise that long-term financial sustainability depends on consistently meeting high standards of corporate responsibility, including on the environment, even if this involves some short-term costs. But in sectors where competition is primarily determined by price -- as in a number of traditional industrial sectors -- there will be a resistance to environmental or other expenditures that might compromise competitiveness.

Other factors important in determining corporate environmental strategies include:

• the perception of environment as a business opportunity;

- requirements established by national environmental policies and regulations, and multilateral agreements;

- willingness and ability to adopt a "pioneer", "defensive" or "follower" position concerning anticipation of, or compliance with, environmental regulations;

- pressures from a range of stakeholders -- consumers, shareholders, financial and insurance institutions and the local community -- to adopt high environmental and social/ethical standards;

- (green) purchaser demands, e.g. from government departments, other companies; and

- corporate image.

Multinational enterprises are at the cutting edge of the corporate environmental response to globalisation. Such enterprises are frequently significant producers of pollution and/or users of natural resources. They are also capable of developing and transferring pollution prevention and control technologies, and they play an important role in diffusing environmental management practices throughout their international operations. Given their market leadership and strong R&D capabilities, they often develop technological and management innovations on their own accord.

A particular challenge is measuring progress towards sustainability. This reflects business managers' concern that "what you cannot measure, you cannot manage". More widely, it also relates to how shareholders and financial institutions evaluate the performance of eco-efficient companies. Developing company-wide indicators of sustainability would be a valuable complement to the conventional indicators of corporate financial performance as shown on balance sheets.

Foreign direct investment -- which continued an upward trend in 1996 to reach a record of around $350 billion, an increase of 10 per cent over 1995, -- will have an important bearing on environmental conditions in many countries. In 1995, the developing countries' share of private capital flows exceeded $167 billion. This compares with the $125 billion of additional assistance to the developing world which, it was estimated at the Rio "Earth Summit", would be needed to promote sustainable development. Thus private capital flows, largely through the activities of multi-national enterprises, are a critical link between the developed and developing world, and a key dimension of globalisation. Equally, the environmental impacts of these investment flows will help to shape the overall environmental impacts of globalisation.

Official development assistance (ODA) is a complement to private capital flows. Increasingly, the challenge will be to promote effective synergy's between them. For example, ODA can help leverage private sector participation in environmental projects and help overcome barriers to foreign direct investment by providing "seed" capital. ODA could also be used to overcome the financing hurdle for environmental investments that are not adequately valued in the market, such as protection of endangered species or habitats.

Small- and medium-sized enterprises (SMEs) comprise a large share of the industry sector in both OECD countries and the DNMEs. For example, in the European Union, SMEs account for 99.8

per cent of business enterprises and provide 95 per cent of total turnover and employment[8] . In Hong Kong, over 95 per cent of the 30,000 factories are SMEs, each typically employing fewer than 50 people[9]; in India, the more than 2 million SMEs account for almost 45 per cent of the country's total industrial output[10].

The pollution load generated by SMEs is significant because of their large number and the diversity of wastes discharged. Many governments accept that SMEs require support, primarily through the provision of information on cleaner technologies and environmental management systems, and are implementing programmes for this purpose. Business is also adopting several measures on its own initiative. Some buyers are requiring their SME suppliers to meet certain environmental specifications in their production and process methods. A number of multinationals are helping their SME suppliers to choose cleaner technologies when new investments are to be made, to redesign products and processes so that they are more environmentally-friendly, and to implement environmental management systems (e.g. EMAS or ISO 14000) and quality assurance standards (ISO 9000). In other cases, multinational enterprises which supply SMEs with feedstocks have agreed to implement a "product stewardship" approach in which the supplier firm collects and disposes of material from its SME customer[11].

Thus, key policy issues include: How is globalisation promoting or impeding improved environmental performance by the business sector? What can the business sector do to optimise the economic and environmental benefits of globalisation? What are the specific challenges and opportunities facing SMEs, and what roles do governments and large businesses have to play to enhance the environmental performance of such enterprises?

Relevant Papers in this Volume

♦ Bjorn Stigson: "Sustainability in an Era of Globalisation: The Business Response" (page 59).

♦ Jih Chang Yang: "Sustainability Challenges in the Information Age" (page 65).

♦ Burton Hamner and Teresita del Rosario: "Green Purchasing: A Channel for Improving the Environmental Performance of SMEs" (page 75).

---

[8]   KPMG Environmental Consulting, 1997: *The Environmental Challenge and Small and Medium-Sized Enterprises in Europe.* KPMG Environmental Consulting. The Hague.

[9]   Lin, C.M., 1997: "Cleaner Production in Small and Medium-Sized Enterprises: The Role of Cleaner Production Programmes" in OECD, 1997: *Cleaner Production in OECD and Dynamic Non-Member Economies.* OECD Proceedings Series. OECD. Paris.

[10]   OECD, 1995: *Technologies for Cleaner Production and Products. Towards Technological Transformation for Sustainable Development.* OECD. Paris.

[11]   OECD, 1995: See Footnote 10.

4.0   Globalisation and the Evolving Role of the State

Deeper trade, investment and capital markets linkages, as well as rapid technological change, have fundamentally changed the environment in which states operate. As a result, the role of the state is shifting from being the principal provider of public goods and services to one of partner, catalyst and facilitator. There is increasing pressure on the state to ensure that its role is matched to its capability (choosing what, and what not, to do, as well as how to do it), and on public institutions to perform their functions more cost-effectively and with greater transparency and accountability.

Environmental governance is becoming more important as a result of globalisation. Increased trade and investment interactions have the potential to amplify existing environmental pressures in the absence of effective and well enforced national environmental policies. At the same time, the intensification of competition associated with globalisation will increase pressure on governments not to imperil the competitiveness of domestic producers by imposing environmental standards on them which are stricter than those faced by foreign competitors (even when "domestic" producers are, in fact, international). This has led some commentators to argue that globalisation will stimulate a "race to the bottom" in environmental standards or the creation of "pollution havens". A more likely scenario, however, is that globalisation will discourage unilateral environmental initiatives and force a convergence around existing environmental standards.

However, "business as usual" will not be an adequate policy response to the environmental trends highlighted at the June 1997 UNGASS meeting. Nor will it be sufficient to encourage significant progress towards sustainable development. Generating the political will to go beyond the *status quo* in environmental standards is clearly crucial. This represents a significant challenge, where further environmental progress will require difficult trade-offs and confrontation with powerful lobby groups. In some DNMEs, the task is complicated by having to deal with three overlapping environmental agendas: problems linked to poverty; the classical range of pollution and natural resource management problems associated with rapid industrialisation; and, the complex set of issues generated by high-income "consumer societies". The prioritisation and sequencing of cost-effective policy responses will therefore be especially important.

Over time, there is likely to be a growing convergence in the national environmental policy agendas of OECD countries and the DNMEs. This will provide a growing mutual interest in policy issues such as:

- streamlining regulatory systems and identifying the most cost-effective environmental policy instruments;

- devising methods to manage environmentally-damaging production and consumption patterns; and

- developing new mechanisms for co-operation with the private sector that go beyond formalistic compliance with statutory requirements and that provide strong incentives for continuous improvements in environmental performance.

Globalisation also has important implications for international environmental governance. The increased attention to the trade, competition and other economic effects of environmental measures underlies demands for clear and equitable international 'rules of the game'. This is evidenced in the debates about the integration of environmental considerations into international trade and investment instruments, as well as in the use of trade sanctions and other economic mechanisms in multilateral environmental agreements. At the same time, environmental issues are receiving considerable attention in regional economic arrangements, e.g. APEC, MERCOSUR and NAFTA.

The nature and context of global environmental problems will also be changed by the process of economic globalisation. The more efficient use of natural resources and wider diffusion of cleaner technologies will be vital in addressing these problems. However, the projected shift in economic weight from OECD to non-OECD countries in the next century will alter the pattern of global and regional environmental pressures and present new challenges in operationalising the principle of "common but differentiated responsibilities".

One element of new public-private sector partnership concerns the provision of environmental goods and services. For example, in the early 1980s, municipal water supply was almost exclusively a public sector responsibility. Since then, it has been privatised or corporatised in a growing number of OECD countries and DNMEs. Similar changes have occurred in other sectors, including telecommunications, mining, public transport and municipal waste management. These changes can yield both economic and environmental benefits by stimulating greater efficiencies in resource allocation and management, and by encouraging new investment. However, new challenges for government also arise, such as establishing and enforcing the legal/regulatory framework necessary to guide private sector operations, and ensuring that essential environmental goods, such as water, are provided in a manner which meets social and economic needs, including those of the poorer sections of society.

Key policy issues include: Is globalisation forcing a convergence around the status quo in environmental policy-making? If so, what types of policy and political initiatives will be needed to meet the environmental challenges posed by globalisation and sustainable development? What types of public-private partnerships seem most promising in terms of optimising financial, environmental and social objectives?

Relevant Papers in this Volume

♦ Tom Burke: "Globalisation, the State and the Environment" (page 91).

♦ Bradford Gentry and Lisa Fernandez: "Evolving Public-Private Partnerships: General Themes and Examples from the Urban Water Sector" (page 99).

5.0 Needs and Opportunities for Shared Analysis and Dialogue

Globalisation can be a positive force in support of sustainable development. At the same time, globalisation is likely to expose more sharply different economic, social and environmental priorities between and within OECD and non-OECD countries.

Maximising the benefits of globalisation and defusing misunderstandings will require further analysis of the environmental implications of globalisation from both OECD Member country and DNME perspectives, as well as closer dialogue and co-operation between these and other groups of countries. Greater emphasis should be given to understanding the national priorities of non-OECD countries and working collaboratively to address them. This would then provide a basis for addressing the more difficult global environmental issues.

Further analysis is needed of specific elements of the globalisation and environment relationship, such as governance, technology, trade and investment, and competitiveness. In this context, participants at the workshop identified several priority issues:

- trade and environment, with particular reference to: (i) deeper analysis of the linkages between production and process methods (PPM) and their environmental impacts; and (ii) increased information exchange and dialogue between OECD Member countries and non-member countries to strengthen the capacity of the latter to participate more fully in the trade and environment debate in international forums such as the WTO Committee on Trade and Environment, UNCTAD and UNEP.

- investment and the environment, focusing on analysis of the environmental implications of portfolio investment and debt finance; the framework conditions required to promote environmentally-sound investment; and the environmental responsibilities of investors.

- new challenges and opportunities for ODA to complement the increased role of private capital flows to emerging economies. Specifically, the role of ODA in leveraging FDI and supporting local environmental programmes or projects which are not valued adequately in the market or which require pump-priming to overcome an initial funding hurdle.

- governance and institutions for environmental management in a globalising economy. Particular emphasis should be placed on mechanisms to strengthen dialogue with business, industry, trade unions, NGOs and other stakeholders. Further analysis of the challenges and opportunities in "mainstreaming" environmental considerations into regional economic arrangements is also needed.

- the social and distributional effects of globalisation and its linkage to the environment. Most work to date has focused on the aggregate social impacts of globalisation on the environment. Analysis of the distributional effects for different groups in society and the spread of environmental (and other) costs and benefits within and between countries is under-researched.

- analysis of the environmental implications of market failures and identifying policy measures to address them. In particular, work could focus on the areas of environmentally-damaging subsidies, internalising environmental costs in commodity prices and promoting markets for "sustainable goods and services".

- environmental management in industry, focusing on analysis and dissemination of "best practices" in public-private sector partnerships and on programmes for integrating environmental management into SMEs. In addition, there is a need to develop indicators of eco-efficiency at the sectoral and industry levels.

ECONOMIC GLOBALISATION AND THE ENVIRONMENT: AN OVERVIEW OF THE LINKAGES

Tom Jones
Environment Directorate, OECD

1.0   Introduction

The purpose of this paper is to provide an overview of the main linkages associated with the globalisation-environment relationship. The paper approaches this goal in two ways. First, it introduces the concept of globalisation and provides an analytical framework for linking that concept to changes in the environment. Second, and drawing on recent OECD work, it identifies the key policy issues underlying each of the main elements in this framework.

2.0   What is Economic Globalisation?

Globalisation can be thought of as a process, with two broad components. First, globalisation causes the structure of markets to change. Markets will generally become both broader (more horizontal integration in production, more consumer access to a wider range of products and services) and deeper (more vertical integration in production, involving new forms of inter-firm co-operation). Second, globalisation will cause the rate of technological change and diffusion to increase. These two components of the globalisation process will also tend to reinforce each other, with a more rapid rate of change in market structure leading to more rapid technological development (and *vice versa*).

The IMF sees the relationship this way (De Jonquières, 1997):

[Globalisation is....] "the growing economic interdependence of countries world-wide through the increasing volume and variety of <u>cross-border transactions in goods and services</u> and of <u>international capital flows</u>, and also through the more rapid and widespread diffusion of <u>technology</u>" (emphasis added).

One of the main ways in which market structures can change is through the "liberalisation" of economic activity. This generally leads to an increased level of competition in the economy. At the international level, it implies the reduction of barriers to the free flow of trade and investment. At the domestic level, it could imply regulatory reforms, and perhaps, increased privatisation. As Wolf (1997) expresses it: "Technology makes globalisation feasible. Liberalisation makes it happen."

Thus, although trade and investment liberalisation and technology change are important parts of the globalisation process, globalisation involves more than just these two elements. From an environmental policy perspective, at least three other dimensions seem important: <u>institutional and</u>

governance issues; sectoral economic activities; and business environmental behaviour. Recent work by the OECD on the globalisation-environment interface has therefore explored all of these themes (see OECD, 1997*a,b*).

It is also useful to think about what globalisation "is not". In particular, globalisation is not the same thing as economic growth. Globalisation contributes to economic growth, but is only one of the contributors. Population change, natural resource endowments, and cultural traditions are other important elements. In making this distinction, however, it is acknowledged that it is very difficult to quantify precisely what proportion of economic growth can be attributed specifically to the globalisation process.

3.0   Globalisation and the Environment: An Analytical Framework

Globalisation is essentially an economic phenomenon, and, like all economic phenomena, it can impact on the environment. In turn, the environment will itself "condition" the globalisation process, by altering both the physical and the political context in which economic activities are carried out.

Globalisation is expected to contribute to the expansion of world economic output (scale effects). It will also generate shifts in the composition and location of production and consumption activities (structural effects). Different technology paths will also be promoted (technology effects), and different product mixes will be produced and consumed (product effects). Each of these changes may generate environmental effects.

The key relationships between globalisation and the environment are often cast in negative terms. For example, environmental costs are often perceived as an extra burden that business has to bear; similarly, environmental needs are often perceived as being sacrificed to business interests. While these negative implications cannot be ignored, it is also important to examine any positive aspects of the globalisation-environment relationship which may exist. For example, proper attention to environmental quality will usually increase total social welfare. It may also be that individual firms prosper most in locations where environmental quality is the highest. It is therefore the net environmental effects of globalisation that should be of interest for policy analysis.

Given the long-term nature of environmental problems, any examination of the environmental consequences of globalisation must be done over a longer time frame than is required for many economic issues. A dynamic and long-term approach is therefore required.

Finally, globalisation refers essentially to the way in which economic variables are changing. These economic changes may, in turn, lead to local, regional or global environmental problems. Global environmental problems (e.g. climate change, ozone depletion) therefore form only one part of the globalisation-environment relationship. The local environmental effects of a globalising economy are also of considerable interest.

Figure 1 illustrates, in a very simplified way, the general structure of the globalisation-environment linkage. Globalisation changes the technology, scale, and composition of production and consumption activities. This generates economic effects (A), which may be either positive or negative for particular actors in the economy. Each of these changes may lead eventually to environmental effects (B). Again, these environmental effects may be either positive or negative. Economic and environmental

18

policies are then introduced (C,D) to offset the negative consequences of each type of effect (or to encourage the positive ones). These policies (hopefully) achieve their goals (E,F). Finally, just as some changes in the economy affect the environment, so also do some changes in the environment affect the economy (G).

Figure 1: Structure of the Globalisation-Environment Linkage

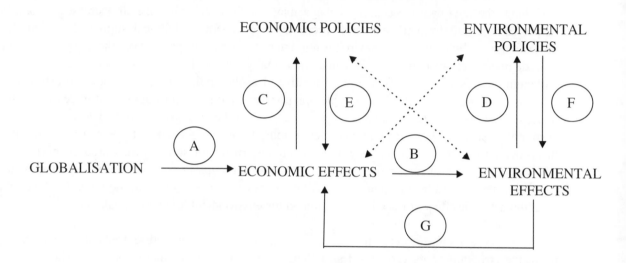

Linkages (A, C, and E) are the essence of the economic policy problem. They are also important to environmental policy-makers, but for different reasons. First, they help describe the conditions surrounding the creation of environmental impacts in the first place. Second, they provide information about the political context in which any environmental policy response must eventually operate. In a sense, they determine which environmental policies are "politically possible". Linkages B, D, F, and G are, of course, the essence of the environmental policy problem.

In summary, the approach taken here is to examine the globalisation-environment linkage from two angles: type of economic activity (trade and investment liberalisation, business behaviour, technology development/diffusion, sectoral economic activities, and governance), and type of impact (scale, composition, technology, and product effects). The following sections are therefore structured along these two axes.

4.0   Trade Issues

Increased international trade (scale effect) is likely to be one key result of globalisation. Trade liberalisation is also likely to lead to shifts in the comparative advantage of some production activities (structural effect), to new technological processes (technology effect), and to shifts in the trade of certain products (product effect). The scale effects are usually assumed to be negative for the environment, and the technology and structural effects are usually assumed to be positive. The primary risk for the environment, therefore, is that the scale effects will be larger than the sum of the technology and structural effects.

Even if there is a negative scale effect, the standard view is that trade policy is not responsible for any associated environmental problems -- these problems stem from inadequate environmental controls on production and consumption activities. Trade is just the vehicle through which these inadequacies are indirectly expressed. Thus, the solution is not to limit trade, but to improve the stringency of environmental policies.

There is also some doubt about the existence of a negative scale effect in the first place. For one thing, the environment-economy linkage may not be a constant one. If increased income levels (expected to result from trade liberalisation) were to generate additional support for environmental protection, thereby reducing the environmental intensity of current production, the negative scale effects of trade liberalisation on the environment could actually turn out to be less than anticipated.
Although there is some empirical support for this idea, the ability of rising incomes to offset the scale effect is by no means certain. For example, the point at which the "uncoupling" of increased trade from increased environmental externalities takes place seems to be at considerably higher income levels than currently exist in many developing countries, leading to the conclusion that the environmental intensity of production in these countries may need to continue rising for some time. Moreover, even if income levels do matter for particular pollutants, and for broad groups of countries over particular periods of time, they may not matter indefinitely, nor for the world as a whole. Overall, therefore, it is not yet clear what the net scale effect of trade liberalisation on the environment might eventually be.

There is some evidence that, once a country begins to industrialise, trade liberalisation helps to make the structure of its economy less pollution-intensive than in those countries whose economies remain relatively closed. In particular, freer trade seems to promote the transition from heavy resource-processing sectors to light manufacturing ones (at least at middle-income levels). One globalisation-related structural shift that has already occurred as a result of trade liberalisation initiatives taken to date is the increased participation of the newly-industrialised economies in the international economy, coupled with their general shift away from primary commodity production, and toward resource-processing, light manufacturing, and service activities. On the other hand, if pollution-intensive production simply shifts to some other country, the world-wide environmental impact may not be reduced at all.

Trade in environmentally-preferred products, particularly eco-efficient capital equipment and its accompanying "clean" production technologies, is another important mechanism through which globalisation may ultimately benefit the environment. For example, trade liberalisation might expand the potential market for less environmentally-intensive final products (e.g. low-emission vehicles). It should also improve access to environmentally-preferable raw material inputs (e.g. low-sulphur coal). Conversely, it could also make environmentally-harmful products (e.g. hazardous substances) or technologies more accessible. (Note, however, that such products do not represent a very large part of total international trade, nor are they necessarily the most serious source of environmental problems.)

Looking at the issue from the reverse perspective ("do environmental policies harm trade?"), most available data suggests that trade flows are likely to be affected only very slightly by even significant changes in the stringency of environmental regulations. For example, world market shares in environmentally-sensitive goods have not changed dramatically over the past two decades, despite the introduction of significantly higher environmental standards in most industrialised countries.

Although it is sometimes politically appealing to link employment reductions in one country with increases in another, there is little empirical evidence that globalisation-related job gains in one country necessarily come at the expense of those lost in another. For example, there has been only a small negative effect on demand for unskilled labour in OECD countries due to trade with non-OECD countries, and that these losses have been largely offset by jobs gained through trade in goods produced by skilled labour.

5.0   Foreign Investment Issues

The scale of global foreign direct investment (FDI) has increased rapidly in recent years, as globalisation has intensified. This may be leading to additional environmental pressures, especially in countries where the environmental policy framework is not adequate, or its implementation is poorly enforced. The structure of this investment is also changing. Flows to the manufacturing sector have generally fallen, in favour of those aimed at the service industries. In principle, these shifts should result in a lessening of environmental pressures, on the assumption that service activities are less environmentally-intensive than manufacturing activities. (This may not always be true, however, given that a full life cycle analysis of services may reveal unexpected environmental consequences.)

On the one hand, most FDI is still occurring within the OECD area, suggesting that much of this capital flow remains subject to the more stringent environmental controls which often exist within OECD countries. On the other hand, large amounts of FDI are still being made in countries where the environmental controls are not always as stringent as the OECD average.

Do countries relax their environmental standards in order to attract new FDI, or to generate a competitive advantage for domestic firms? Do industries actually disinvest in countries with higher environmental standards, and if so, are environmental costs the reason for this disinvestment? Does this tactic pay off in terms of long-run economic competitiveness? Available evidence suggests that the answer to all of these questions is usually "no", even though local exceptions are often noted.

For example, there is little evidence of widespread "pollution havens" in the global economy. There are some industries, in some countries, where this conclusion does not hold, but this is not the general case. Most actual shifts in investments can be attributed to structural adjustments, rather than to the presence of lower environmental standards *per se*. In fact, pollution havens seem to be more often associated with protectionist economies than they are with environmentally-tolerant ones. If anything, available evidence suggests that the imposition of higher environmental standards will tend to generate a technological response, rather than leading to capital flights.

At least three types of FDI can be distinguished -- "market-seeking" (where the purpose of the investment is to ensure access to the market of the destination country); "resource-seeking" (where the investment is made to ensure more reliable supplies of natural resources); and "platform-seeking" (where the purpose of the investment is to provide a "platform" for production and/or sales activities in a regional market. Where pollution havens do exist, they are more likely to be associated with "resource-seeking" FDI than with either of the other two types.

Despite the relatively sparse evidence of pollution havens, most companies are prepared to use the threat of industrial relocation as a way of reducing environmental burdens on their operations. This threat is sometimes real enough to convince policy-makers not to impose new environmental regulations, or to reduce the stringency of ones which already exist.

In-coming FDI will often lead to increased employment, which is one reason why many governments are willing to accept these investments. It also explains why FDI-source countries are so nervous about the mobility of capital in a more globalised economy. It is therefore particularly important in the latter countries to explain the employment effects of globalisation in general equilibrium terms. Often, reductions in employment due to investments made elsewhere are part of a larger trend toward a more efficient economic structure—one that actually offers increased employment opportunities in the home country, and is less environmentally-intensive in the bargain.

Because FDI flows are most likely to involve "greenfield" investments, they are the component of total financial flows that is usually regarded as being most important for the environment. However, portfolio investments and debt instruments still constitute the largest proportion of total financial flows. When viewed from a life-cycle perspective, these instruments could also represent larger implications for the environment than originally anticipated. In effect, the environmental consequences of these latter flows may be more subtle, but just as real, as the environmental impacts of FDI itself.

6.0   Business Issues

The business community is likely to be in the "front line" of any environmental response to economic globalisation. The way business responds to the challenge of globalisation will therefore make a big difference to the achievement of environmental goals. Environmental policies are also likely to be increasingly prominent elements of business strategies.

From the business perspective, companies are rapidly extending the geographical range of their activities, and increasingly have to respond to the environmental requirements of governments other than "their own". From the government perspective, modern trading rules require national governments to treat an increasingly foreign-based business community in the same way that domestic firms are treated, when national environmental policies are developed.

Much of the focus in globalisation-environment discussions centres around the role played by the Multinational Enterprises (MNEs). MNEs are often significant polluters and/or users of natural resources. They also maintain relatively high levels of R&D expenditure, and are capable of transferring pollution abatement technologies across international frontiers.

On the other hand, the Small and Medium Enterprises (SMEs) are much more numerous, and therefore more difficult to manage, from an environmental perspective. They also generate a significant number of environmental problems in their own right. As these firms become more international in their outlooks, these problems may intensify. Special efforts therefore need to be made to understand the environmental needs, constraints, and opportunities associated with this group.

Globalisation is heightening the influence of wider stakeholder interests over the formulation of business strategies (including environmental strategies). These interests take the form of various pressures transmitted to the company from its "multiple stakeholder" groups, including regulators, consumers, insurers, trading partners, employees, and environmental non-governmental organisations. Each of these groups has its own environmental agenda, and each is sometimes in a position to influence business environmental behaviour.

The business community seems to be implementing its international environmental strategies in one of two basic ways: the <u>devolved</u> approach (in which environmental standards are met on a country-by-country basis), and the <u>centralised</u> approach (in which a single standard is adopted for the global operations of the enterprise -- generally, this standard reflects the environmental policies existing in the most stringent nation). Available evidence suggests some recent shifts in the direction of the centralised approach, although this is by no means universal. To the extent that this represents the spread of the best-available technologies, it may have some positive long-term implications for the environment.

Much of the discussion about corporate environmental behaviour centres around how to exploit "win-win" opportunities (i.e. where both corporate profits and environmental quality are enhanced). However, the real challenge is not to persuade companies to pursue these "win-win" strategies (which they will probably do in any event), but to persuade them to pursue environmental goals even when short-term profitability may seem likely to be compromised.

Profitability is directly linked to competitiveness issues, which of course, lie at the heart of the globalisation-environment relationship. In this regard, the competitiveness of individual firms is the most important political question that needs to be addressed.

There are two potential problems here. Either a firm's competitiveness may be compromised by environmental policies that impose unacceptable economic hardships (an economic concern), or pressure might grow to reduce the strength and/or effectiveness of environmental policies (an environmental concern).

There are two potential opportunities here as well. First, reduced competitiveness at the level of the firm is sometimes more than offset by increased competitiveness at the level of the economy (or in other firms who profit from the shift). These "general equilibrium" benefits need to be emphasised in the policy debates about globalisation and competitiveness. Second, an increasing number of firms are recognising that their competitiveness is not always negatively affected by higher standards of environmental performance. Sometimes the cost of environmental policies is not significant enough to reduce competitiveness; sometimes there are even positive effects in the form of "first mover" advantages, such as technology access and market dominance. These positive implications need to be fully explored and promoted.

In general, the more flexible environmental policies are, the more likely the business community will be to support them. In the long run, a co-operative approach to environmental improvements, involving business in partnership with governments, is likely to be a key feature of a more globalised economy.

7.0   Technology Issues

Globalisation is generally expected to lead to higher rates of technology development and diffusion. By increasing the size of the market, globalisation provides firms with greater incentives to innovate (since they will realise even greater profits from successful innovations than would have been the case in the absence of trade). For those technological developments which require large production runs to be efficient, diffusion rates may also increase. Higher rates of technology development and diffusion are generally expected to reduce pressure on the environment (i.e. a positive technology effect).

Globalisation is also expected to reduce the costs of given technologies at the level of the individual firm. These reduced costs should make it easier for firms to apply environmentally-friendly "process integration" technologies, and allow them to move away from environmentally-less-friendly "add-on" approaches to pollution control or resource extraction.

Finally, globalisation should facilitate the spread of so-called "clean technologies", as part of the structural shifts associated with economic integration at the level of the firm. For example, MNEs can play a significant role in influencing the technological characteristics of domestic firms either through "reverse engineering", or by promoting common technical standards world-wide. Most observers therefore assume that international investment flows will result in the application of less environmentally-damaging technologies.

The environmental goods and services industry is another vehicle through which environmentally-beneficial technologies might be spread. Global sales of pollution abatement equipment and related services have expanded rapidly in recent years.

At the national level, technology development paths will be partially determined by a country's capacity to absorb new innovations, and partly by its inherent natural resource endowments. For these reasons, it is not surprising that it is the OECD countries which have benefited most so far from the technological advances inherent in the globalisation process. Some of the newly-industrialising countries have also benefited from international flows in knowledge and technology, particularly in the so-called "mid-tech" sectors, but except for some the simpler technologies (e.g. textiles), the developing countries are not yet fully participating in these benefits.

8.0   Sectoral Issues

Globalisation is likely to lead to lower freight costs across most transport modes in most countries. For example, the World Bank (1997) reports that the real cost of sea freight fell by nearly 70% between 1980 and 1986. Air freight rates showed similar declines. Even where transport costs may rise in the short term, the longer-term pressure on costs is still likely to be downwards.

Reduced costs, combined with the increased incomes that should result from a more efficient transport system, are likely to result in new demands for transport services (scale effects), in modal switches (structural effects), or in the spread of new transportation technologies (technology effects). Opportunities for transport cost reductions will also encourage firms to shift their production and marketing activities to locations where these opportunities can best be exploited. This structural shift will probably have political implications in both the old and the new locations.

Competition associated with globalisation is also intensifying the search for ways of reducing energy costs, especially the costs of electricity. Many countries have therefore recently eased restrictions on electricity generation activities. Deregulation and privatisation of electricity production (structural effects) are thus intensifying the pressure to use cheaper fuels, or to use energy more efficiently.

24

Globalisation is also expected to lead to two broad shifts in the <u>agriculture</u> sector: increased pressure to liberalise the trade in agricultural products, and increased pressure to reform domestic agricultural policies, in order to retain the competitiveness of national agriculture.

Once again, the environmental consequences of these changes may be positive or negative, depending on the particular circumstances. For example, the negative scale effects of reduced transport costs are likely to be higher than average in the "transit" countries. Globalisation-induced structural shifts could also conceivably harm the environment (by encouraging shifts to the road mode), or help the environment (by increasing the efficiency of back-hauls and/or routing patterns).

Similarly, trade liberalisation might decrease farm-gate prices in some countries, imperiling some of the environmental benefits currently being generated by farmers (e.g. countryside management benefits). On the other hand, trade reform also implies that agricultural activity might become more extensive than at present, perhaps generating additional environmental benefits (e.g. in the form of reduced need for chemical fertilisers).

9.0 Governance Issues

Some observers anticipate that globalisation will ultimately lead to a reduced role for the nation state. In this view, the increased transferability of economic resources (especially capital and technology) will reduce the power of nation states to control environmental activities within their jurisdictions. If an individual state were to enact "overly aggressive" environmental rules, capital flights to less-demanding states could occur.

Not everyone is convinced that the role of national governments will decline in a more globalised economy. In this view, national governments will remain the key players in the world governance system. National governments are still the basis for all forms of international co-operation; they also still legitimise all domestic activities. As Hirst and Thompson (1995) put it: "...The state may no longer be able to impose outcomes on all dimensions of policy, but it will remain a key institution in sustaining governance of the international economy. ... It will make international agreements stick, upwards because it represents a territory, and downwards because it is a constitutionally-legitimate power."

From an environmental perspective, most environmental resources will never be capable of being effectively priced. An efficient economy and a sustainable environment will therefore continue to require at least two forms of government intervention—one to set the operating rules through which economic transactions take place (contribution to sustainable <u>growth</u>); the other to ensure that market failures do not lead to long-term environmental degradation (contribution to sustainable <u>development</u>).

Of course, these functions could be performed by some other level of government than the national one. But several things point to the idea that the national government will still be relevant in a more globalised economic context. For one thing, national governments have considerable experience in addressing local environmental externalities, and local externalities will still exist, despite the globalisation process. It may be that national governments have less competence in dealing with regional and global externalities, or with local externalities which have significant implications for international competitiveness. There may therefore be eventually a role for other levels of government to play in these latter issues, but there is still no form of regional or global governance that is not based on national governments.

Globalisation also represents increased challenges (and increased opportunities) for regional and global institutions to better integrate environmental and economic objectives. For example, it will be increasingly important to ensure that international financial/economic institutions (e.g. World Bank, EBRD, IADB) and trade organisations (e.g. WTO) take due account of environmental concerns in their work, and that international environmental organisations (e.g. UNEP) take due account of competitiveness concerns in theirs.

It may also be possible to think of new "sub-global" institutional solutions to environmental problems, based on multilateral agreements among key geo-political groups. Regional economic institutions probably have a key role to play here. Many environmental problems have more relevance at the regional scale than they do at the local or global levels. It is also noted that most international trade and investment today occurs within economic regions, rather than between them. Opportunities may therefore exist for integrating environmental and economic objectives at the regional level in ways that are not possible at the local or global levels.

The OECD countries have a special contribution to make in this context. Not only does this group constitute one of the key actors in the globalisation-environment relationship (the developed countries), it also has regular links to the other main actor (the developing and newly-industrialising countries), through its outreach activities. Furthermore, one of the fundamental missions of the OECD is the reconciliation of environmental and economic policies.

Competitiveness concerns associated with globalisation are likely to lead to a certain amount of "convergence" in environmental policies. This convergence will be most pronounced among countries whose markets are highly integrated, and relatively homogeneous. Since these are key characteristics of the OECD country group, the implication is that some OECD environmental policies may converge around an "OECD average". Some developing country and DNME environmental policies may also be pulled toward the OECD average, as their economies become more deeply integrated with those of the OECD. This implies that leadership by OECD countries in establishing appropriate environmental standards will be especially important.

What kind of leadership is required? Globalisation implies a need for more efficient forms of international co-operation in all areas of economic activity. This applies as much to activities related to the environment, as it does to any other element of economic activity. The OECD might therefore contribute to improving the quality of this international co-operation.

In principle, government interventions should be made at the same level as the environmental externality that is of concern. Thus, local externalities should generally be addressed by local responses; national ones by national responses; and global ones should generally be addressed at the global level. The problem with this approach is that in a more globalised economy, the boundaries between environmental effects (externalities) and economic effects (especially competitiveness problems) will become less distinct. Local environmental effects will increasingly have international economic consequences, and global environmental problems will increasingly generate local economic impacts. This implies that there may be no such thing as a truly "national" environmental externality.

If this is so, at least three types of government intervention may be warranted: (i) national policies to internalise the environmental costs of those domestic externalities which have <u>no</u> international competitiveness implications; (ii) co-operative arrangements with other governments on common policies to address those domestic environmental externalities which <u>do</u> have international competitiveness implications; and (iii) co-operative arrangements for addressing transfrontier/global environmental externalities.

The first case involves only national policies, and is not dealt with further here. The latter two cases imply some form of multilateral co-operation. This co-operation would have two important characteristics: (i) it would not necessarily target international environmental externalities; it could also cover domestic externalities where significant international competitiveness concerns exist; and (ii) it would not necessarily involve all countries. As noted earlier, many environmental (and competitiveness) problems have more relevance at the regional scale than they do at the global level.

International co-operation of the type suggested here could take various forms (binding and enforceable commitments, voluntary actions, codes of conduct, guidelines, etc.). The more binding the commitment, the more nations will probably regard the agreement as a possible infringement on their sovereignty. There is no particular need for the international co-operation to be limited to governments. It could, for example, involve co-operation at the level of the international business community to achieve shared environmental goals. For example, the chemicals industry has successfully instituted a "Responsible Care" Programme among its members.

10.0   Conclusions

Largely via the processes of trade and investment liberalisation, globalisation will generate scale, structural, technology, and product impacts on environment. These effects may be positive or negative, depending on circumstances. Although not enough is yet known about the precise nature of these effects, the suspicion is that the scale effects will be largely negative for the environment, and the structural and technology effects will be largely positive. The challenge for governments will be to find ways of maximising the positive environmental consequences, while limiting the negative ones.

In attempting to do so, governments will find that longer-term environmental goals often conflict with shorter-term economic competitiveness goals. On the other hand, there are probably situations where environmental policies are actually beneficial for competitiveness, employment, and economic growth (e.g. through the dynamics of technology development).

Where the environmental effects are negative, the reasons for this will often have more to do with failings in environmental policies than with failings in economic ones. If anything, therefore, globalisation is likely to intensify the need for stronger environmental policies, rather than to reduce it. Given the increasing internationalisation of environmental problems, and of the economic competitiveness problems associated with these problems, a stronger environmental regime will inevitably require more international co-operation.

National governments and the business community will each have a key role to play in ensuring that this co-operation occurs, even though neither has a lot of experience in this area. Some creative thinking on both sides is therefore required.

REFERENCES

DE JONQUIÈRES, G. (1997): "Reform Has Not Yet Gone Far Enough" in "Is Globalisation Inevitable and Desirable?" Internet @ http://www.monde-diplomatique.fr/md/dossiers/ft/.

HIRST, P. and THOMPSON, G. (1995): "Globalisation and the Future of the Nation State" in Economy and Society(24)3, pp. 408-442.

OECD (1997*a*): *Globalisation and the Environment: Preliminary Perspectives*. OECD. Paris.

OECD (1997*b*): *Economic Globalisation and the Environment*. OECD. Paris.

WOLF, M. (1997): "Why This Hatred of the Market?" in "Is Globalisation Inevitable and Desirable?" Internet @ http://www.monde-diplomatique.fr/md/dossiers/ft/.

WORLD BANK (1997): Global Economic Prospects and the Developing Countries 1997. The World Bank. Washington D.C.

BEYOND UNGASS: CHALLENGES FOR OECD AND DYNAMIC NON-MEMBER ECONOMIES

Derek Osborn
Environmental Policy Consultant, United Kingdom and Co-Chair "Earth Summit+5" Negotiations

1.0   Sustainable Development

Thirty years ago the Club of Rome argued that if we have excessive numbers of people on the planet, consuming excessive resources and producing excessive pollution the world would be in dire straits. They postulated the need for zero growth. Subsequently this came to seem too alarmist to most people. The world's natural resources seemed to be more extensive than previously assessed and pollution seemed to be manageable with appropriate policies and technology. Indeed, many of the world's environmental problems appeared easier to solve if economic growth first provided the wherewithal to tackle them.

Out of this debate came the concept of sustainable development -- the path of virtuous economic growth coupled with good environmental practice that hands on to future generations a world as good as or better than the one we inherit.

2.0   The 1992 Rio "Earth Summit"

The 1992 Rio "Earth Summit" was arguably the high point of that optimistic line of thought -- the apotheosis of sustainable development. Two major conventions were signed by heads of state and Agenda 21 purported to establish a comprehensive blueprint for the kind of actions needed by governments and others to achieve a sustainable path for development in the future.

3.0   UNGASS "Earth Summit+5"

At the UN General Assembly Special Session (UNGASS) in June 1997 (otherwise known as the "Earth Summit+5" or "Earth Summit II") the prospects looked less favourable. The relevance and importance of Agenda 21 and the concept of sustainable development were reaffirmed. However, it was widely acknowledged that progress in meeting the commitments made at the 1992 Rio "Earth Summit" was very uneven. Of greater concern was that the political will to making development more sustainable seemed perceptibly weaker.

The purpose of the Special Session was first to take stock of progress since the Rio "Earth Summit"; second, to review the adequacy of the international institutional machinery and resources for promoting sustainable development and; third, to put new initiatives in place where existing arrangements were considered unsatisfactory or incapable of delivering the desired results.

The UNGASS Assessment

Analytical reports prepared for UNGASS showed that on most measures environmental conditions world-wide have worsened since 1992, and that general trends are not sustainable. For example, UNEP's 1997 Global Environment Outlook 1 report[1] noted that, *inter alia*,:

- greenhouse gases are still being emitted at levels higher than the stabilisation goal agreed upon under the UN Framework Convention on Climate Change;

- the use of renewable resources, such as land, fisheries, forests, fresh water, is beyond their natural regeneration capacity and thus unsustainable;

- rapid, unplanned urbanisation, especially in coastal areas, is placing major stress on adjacent ecosystems;

- changes to global biogeochemical cycles are leading to widespread acidification, changes in hydrological cycles and the loss of biodiversity, biomass and bioproductivity.

At the same time the pressures which humankind is placing on the world's carrying capacity is increasing. Populations are still growing in most countries. Consumption per capita is also steadily trending up.

In New York in February 1997, delegates to the UN Commission for Sustainable Development (UN CSD) meeting agreed that five subjects merited particular effort and attention:

- the need to combat poverty and growing inequality among countries, with a focus on assisting further the poorest countries which have yet to receive the benefits of economic growth elsewhere and the process of globalisation. Poverty in these countries exacerbates, and is exacerbated by, their environmental problems such as deforestation, drought, desertification and soil erosion;

- freshwater, in particular the need to bring clean water and sanitation to the hundreds of millions of people who lack access to these services at present. At the same time, increased attention is needed to define strategies to deal with the longer-term problems of dwindling freshwater resources and increasing pollution of water supplies in many parts of the world;

- the global atmosphere and the need for a clear strategy to deal with climate change (together with the related issues of transport and energy). At the regional and local levels, air pollution remains a major problem;

---

[1]   UN Environment Programme, 1997: *Global Environment Outlook 1. Global State of the Environment Report 1997.* Oxford University Press. New York.

- forests, specifically the urgency of establishing an effective on-going process to promote the sustainable management of forests world-wide; and

- the oceans, especially the importance of strengthened international co-operation and political impetus to halt the severe decline in fish stocks in many parts of the world resulting from over-fishing.

The hope and the expectation of some when the process started in February 1997 was that by the time of the April meeting of the UN CSD and UNGASS in June that year, countries would have taken up these issues in their capitals and brought forward concrete proposals for making significant progress on them as well as the many other issues identified in the pre-UNGASS period.

Some made strong efforts to move the process forward. The European Union in particular tried hard on the environment side with new initiatives on fresh water, energy, a vigorous campaign to begin negotiations on a convention to protect the world's forests and a forward position on climate change in preparation for the December 1997 Kyoto Conference of the Parties to the UN Framework Convention on Climate Change.

Critically, countries were unable to come forward with new proposals on the development side. The sense of unfulfilled expectations since Rio on the part of developing countries deepened. At Rio developing countries thought they were being promised more official development assistance (ODA) to help them make the transition to sustainable development; instead five years later, ODA levels have declined sharply from 0.34% of GNP to 0.27% of GNP. Private capital flows have to some extent filled the gap but these flows have been going only to a small number of developing countries. For the majority of these countries ODA remains very important.

4.0   The UNGASS Outcome

The failure and inability of the developed countries to come forward with new proposals on development assistance meant that the mood at the end of the Special Session was sombre. Indeed, it proved impossible to agree any final declaration by heads of state to embody the political commitment of all countries to a partnership for sustainable development.

Nevertheless, the Special Session did agree to a more detailed assessment of progress since Rio and a Programme for the Further Implementation of Agenda 21. On the environment side there was some advance. For example, there was limited commitment to developing more sustainable energy and transport policies over the next few years; freshwater is to be the sectoral theme of the 1998 UN CSD work programme; and there was clear recognition of the need for vigorous action to halt over-fishing in the oceans.

These negotiated agreements have so far lacked the oxygen of publicity and the strength of political commitment, however. This implies that there is unlikely to be concerted effort to implement them with new binding international agreements or the deployment of additional resources. In addition, nothing was done to strengthen the international institutional machinery to promote sustainable development.

Needs for the Future

Achieving sustainable development will involve much bigger changes than we have seen so far. For example:

- stabilising greenhouse gas emissions and eventually concentrations will require large reductions in the consumption of fossil fuels, with important implications for energy supply and energy efficiency strategies. Major changes in lifestyles, in people's homes and above all in their transport habits will also be called for;

- protecting the world's oceans and forests will require them to be managed in ways quite different to that practised at present with greater emphasis on harvesting sustainable yields;

- consumption patterns will need to change and recycling of waste products on a much larger scale will be necessary;

- population growth will need to slow further.

Such changes cannot be achieved by governments acting alone. They will have to involve everyone and every part of society: industry and farmers, scientists and teachers, municipal government and local communities, etc. Above all, individual people and families have to be engaged.

5.0   Towards the "Earth Summit+10" in 2002

It was not unexpected that the world shied away from deeper commitment at UNGASS in 1997. The underlying issues will not go away, however, and looking ahead the international community needs to consider how the situation could be transformed by the time of the "Earth Summit+10" in the year 2002. This will be a bigger day of reckoning that the five-year staging post of 1997, and it will be crucial to have built up by then a more effective international partnership between developed and developing countries in support of sustainable development.

Sustainable development remains essential -- the strategic overarching concept to guide countries towards meeting their environmental, social and economic goals in the new century. But it will not be achieved by drift and hoping for the best.

Opportunities for moving the sustainable agenda forward must be seized. For example, a review of the 1995 Copenhagen Summit on Social Development is scheduled for the year 2000, where issues of social injustice, aid and poverty will head the agenda. The UN Secretary-General's Reform proposals have also canvassed the possibility of a Millennial General Assembly in 2000 which could be a further opportunity for reviewing the objectives and functions of the UN, including promoting sustainable development.

A Strategy Leading Up To 2002

It will be important to establish as soon as possible a coherent strategy for the next five years so that by the year 2002 there is indeed real progress to report. Establishing realistic expectations, a comprehensive schedule of preparatory events and a clear political commitment to effective follow-up and implementation will be a key part of ensuring success.

The multi-year work programme now established for the annual meetings of the UN CSD provides a focal point (see Annex I). The programme establishes an orderly sequence for examining topics in a structured manner, with different subjects allocated to different years so that the UN CSD can avoid the over-ambitious task of trying to deal with every one every year and ending up doing so only in a superficial way.

The Importance of Building Political Awareness and Momentum

Fulfillment of the UN CSD's work programme cannot on its own ensure the progress that is needed. Mobilisation of political and public support throughout the world is also required.

In this context the key achievement of Rio was not the texts of Agenda 21 and the other agreements. It was the process of mobilising and responding to public awareness of the issues and an expressed popular demand for action locally, nationally and internationally. The momentum for this process gathered speed over several years culminating at Rio. The Brundtland report on "Our Common Future" presented credible, persuasive analysis and gave a high level political lead. A series of regional conferences before Rio helped to define issues and expectations, and innumerable local and national meetings and discussions built up the pressure further.

Such a process cannot be manufactured. It has to feed on real environmental problems and genuine public concern about them. That concern continues to be present among the public, as many surveys have shown. What it lacks is focus. NGOs and governmental and international forums can help to ensure that public concern becomes articulated and heard in a coherent way so that a popular consensus about problems and possible solutions supports and motivates politicians and officials engaged in the detailed shaping of national policies and negotiation of international agreements. The two year period of preparation and consciousness-raising for Rio also meant that the public and politicians could reach out to each other across national boundaries, understand better each other's views, and help to influence the positions which their own countries were taking in the interests of securing a consensus.

It was this process of public discussion and debate which was conspicuously missing in the lead up to the UNGASS "Earth Summit+5". Lack of time and to some extent "conference-fatigue" amongst some of the principal players and in the UN itself were some of the reasons behind this.

Looking towards the "Earth Summit+10" in 2002 it is clear that a coherent political and popular process of engagement, particularly in the period 2000 to 2002, will be necessary to secure effective results. The 1997 UNGASS was a warning signal that the post-Rio process and Agenda 21 have been going astray and that concerted effort and commitment will be needed in the years ahead to put them back on course.

Up to 2002 two periods of activity might be distinguished. First, up to 2000 and the Millennial Assembly in that year the key themes and ideas could be identified and debated. Possibly a new Commission on the lines of the Brundtland Commission could have a role to play in this phase. Second, between 2000 and 2002 a more focused debate and negotiation would bring some of the key issues to the point of decision.

Some Candidates for Agreement in 2002

On the basis of the 1997 UNGASS, four candidate areas stand out for substantive agreement in or by 2002.

First, climate change. Although the US, Europe and Japan agreed differentiated targets applying to themselves at the 1997 Kyoto Conference of the Parties to the UN Framework Convention on Climate Change, more needs to be done. To establish an early expectation that there will be another major Summit in 2002 and that heads of state will be looking to substantive outcomes from it could help catalyse the same sort of breakthrough as Rio helped to achieve in the negotiation of the framework climate change convention.

Second, forests. An interim process was established at UNGASS which includes the identification of possible elements of a forest convention to be negotiated sometime in the future. Although there continues to be considerable anxiety in some countries about the idea of a convention, on the grounds of loss of sovereignty and other reasons, there does also appear to be growing recognition of the importance of sustainable management of forests and the possibility that an international agreement may facilitate effective ways to achieve this. The development of a convention might therefore become an achievable goal for 2002. It could be coupled with the ambition to turn the Convention on Biological Diversity into a stronger instrument for protecting biodiversity, particularly tropical forest ecosystems.

Third, freshwater. The debates on this subject at the UN CSD in 1997 were one of the few encouraging areas where there was commonality of concern and recognition that progress internationally could be made. The developed countries agreed that part of the UN CSD's new work mandate must focus on establishing practical programmes and mobilising fresh resources, recognising that better access to water and sanitation is one of the most practical and effective approaches to poverty alleviation. If the programme that is to be developed further in a series of meetings during 1998 is sufficiently robust and credible, it could lead to substantive agreements by the year 2002 on strategies to promote the sustainable management of freshwater.

Finally, the oceans and the issue of over-fishing. Hitherto it has usually been argued that this issue was best addressed at the regional rather than international level. That view may continue to prevail. However, given the similarity of over-fishing problems in different parts of the world and the increasing influence of a limited number of major fishing fleets, a broader international agreement may well be needed in the future.

A New Deal on Development

To ensure a successful "Earth Summit+10" it will be essential to reinforce efforts to secure a new deal on the financial issues. Some rapidly industrialising countries will be moving beyond the need for aid from developed countries but for others poverty and environmental degradation will be more acute than ever. There is a clear need for a reversal of the downward trend in ODA, increased debt relief, timely replenishment of the Global Environment Facility (GEF) and further financial resources to implement the desertification convention.

In the Dynamic Non-Member Economies (DNMEs), local and foreign investment will likely continue to be the main engines of economic growth. The DNMEs and OECD countries share a common interest in ensuring that private capital flows help promote rather than impede sustainable development.

These are difficult tasks which will require the definition and implementation of coherent long-term strategies operating at all levels -- local, national, international -- and covering the public and private sectors. Governments will need to produce more balanced sustainable development strategies, with the social, environmental and economic dimensions all given appropriate weight. Local government will need to commit to implementing Local Agenda 21s, an area where there has been commendable progress in many parts of the world. Industry will have to develop further its ability to deliver sustainable growth through eco-efficiency and other approaches.

The UN CSD and UNGASS have made some progress in establishing dialogues with all the major groups at international level to help identify the roles that the different stakeholders can play and the support they require from national governments and the provisions of international agreements. Nonetheless, much remains to be done. The position of the DNMEs, in particular their views on the international initiatives and agreements needed to further promote sustainable development will be crucial since they are key partners and brokers in any agreement that might be forged between the OECD countries and the G77.

In addition to the environmental issues identified earlier, other key sustainability issues for the relationship between OECD countries and the DNMEs include:

- access to information about the environment and the environmental impacts of development between and within countries;

- the role of environmental standards and the extent to which they can be harmonised;

- the linkages among trade, investment and the environment and the extent to which common rules and standards are appropriate; and

- the role of environmentally-sound technologies and the extent to which globalisation can further facilitate its transfer.

6.0   Conclusions

A new deal and substantive agreements on sustainability in 2002 will depend crucially on the relationship between OECD countries and the DNMEs. In particular, their ability to find common ground on the issues discussed in this paper. They clearly have a mutual interest in doing so, and in beginning together the process of building political awareness and momentum towards a successful "Earth Summit+10" in 2002. This offers the prospect of moving from the present position of "SLUDGE" (Slightly Less Unsustainable Development Genuflecting to the Environment) to that of "DREAMS" (Development Reconciling Environmental and Material Success).

Annex I: Multi-Year Programme of Work for the Commission on Sustainable Development, 1998-2002 as endorsed at UNGASS

1998 Session: Over-riding issues: Poverty, consumption and production patterns		
Sectoral Theme: Strategic Approaches to Freshwater Management. Review of outstanding chapters of the Programme of Action for the Sustainable Development of Small Island Developing States[a]	Cross-sectoral Theme: Transfer of Technology/Capacity-Building/Education/Science/Awareness-Raising	Economic Sector/Major Group: Industry
Main issues for an integrated discussion under the above theme: Agenda 21, chapters 2-8, 10-15, 18-21, 23-34, 36, 37, 40	Main issues for an integrated discussion under the above theme: Agenda 21, chapters 2-4, 6, 16, 23-37, 40	Main issues for an integrated discussion under the above theme: Agenda 21, chapters 4, 6, 9, 16, 17, 19-21, 23-35, 40

1999 Session: Over-riding issues: Poverty, consumption and production patterns		
Comprehensive review of the Programme of Action for the Sustainable Development of Small Island Developing States		
Sectoral Theme: Oceans and Seas	Cross-sectoral Theme: Consumption and Production Patterns	Economic Sector/Major Group: Tourism
Main issues for an integrated discussion under the above theme: Agenda 21, chapters 5-7, 9, 15, 17, 19-32, 34-36, 39-40	Main issues for an integrated discussion under the above themes: Agenda 21, chapters 2-10, 14, 18-32, 34-36, 40	Main issues for an integrated discussion under the above themes: Agenda 21, chapters 2-7, 13, 15, 17, 23-33, 36

---

[a]   Review to include those chapters of the SIDS Programme of Action not covered in the in-depth review carried out by the fourth session of the UN CSD.

2000 Session: Over-riding issues: Poverty, consumption and production patterns		
Sectoral Theme: Integrated Planning and Management of Land Resources	Cross-sectoral Theme: Financial Resources/Trade and Investment/Economic Growth	Economic Sector/Major Group: Agriculture[b] Day of Indigenous People
Main issues for an integrated discussion under the above theme: Agenda 21, chapters 2-8, 10-37, 40	Main issues for an integrated discussion under the above theme: Agenda 21, chapters 2-4, 23-33, 36-38, 40	Main issues for an integrated discussion under the above theme: Agenda 21, chapters 2-7, 10-16, 18-21, 23-34, 37, 40

2001 Session: Over-riding issues: Poverty, consumption and production patterns		
Sectoral Theme: Atmosphere; Energy	Cross-sectoral Theme: Information for Decision-Making and Participation International Co-operation for an Enabling Environment	Economic Sector/Major Group: Energy; Transport
Main issues for an integrated discussion under the above theme: Agenda 21, chapters 4, 6-9, 11-14, 17, 23-37, 39-40	Main issues for an integrated discussion under the above theme: Agenda 21, chapters 2, 4, 6, 8, 23-36, 38-40	Main issues for an integrated discussion under the above theme: Agenda 21, chapters 2-5, 8, 9, 20, 23-37, 40

2002 Session
Comprehensive review

---

[b]   Including forestry.

GLOBALISATION, ENVIRONMENTALISM AND NEW TRANSNATIONAL SOCIAL FORCES

Eduardo Viola
Department of International Relations and Centre for Sustainable Development,
University of Brasilia, Brazil

1.0   Introduction

This paper is structured in three parts. First, I analyse the fundamental characteristics of the process of globalisation and its multiple dimensions: military, economic, financial, communications, religious, interpersonal, scientific-technical, population and migration, environmental, epidemiological, criminal and political. Second, I examine the socio-political impact of the emergence and development of different types of environmentalism. In the final part of the paper, I focus on several major developments in global environmental governance.

2.0   From the International to the Transnational and the Multiple Dimensions of Globalisation

The second half of the 1980s was a period in which the process of globalisation intensified as a greater number of countries became more active participants in the world economy. The political implosion between 1989 and 1991 in central and eastern Europe and the former Soviet Union that signaled the end of the Cold War added to that process.

In this section I discuss the main features of the globalisation process and its multiple dimensions. Although what follows is a personal conceptualisation and classification, I acknowledge the inspiration of the following: Caldwell (1990), Guidens (1990), North (1990), Rosenau (1990), Sand (1990), Buzan (1991), Fossaert (1991), MacNeill, Winsemius and Yakushiji (1991), Porter and Brown (1991), Cairncross (1992), Hurrell and Kingsbury (1992), Stern, Young and Druckman (1992), Kennedy (1993), Morin and Kern (1993), Brown et al. (1995 and 1996), Commission on Global Governance (1995), Held (1995), Risse-Kappen (1995), Zolo (1995) and Werksman (1996).

To provide a framework for the discussion some organising ideas are presented here. First, the world is shrinking metaphorically-speaking through, for example, wider access to and use of information technologies, the growing trade and investment linkages among countries, the growth in cross-border business alliances and mergers and acquisitions, and the spread of product brand names recognisable world-wide. However, globalisation is not homogenisation. The limits between the national and international are increasingly blurred as is the differentiation between internal-external linkages within individual countries.

Second, there is a movement from the international to the transnational/global system in international relations. The international system was state-centric. The transnational/global system is simultaneously state-centric (not hegemonic) and multi-centric (high diversity of social forces and actors, such as multi-national corporations, NGOs, inter-governmental organizations, industry and issue-specific interest groups and media opinion-formers).

Third, there is a new dynamic in the microsocial-macrosocial relationship. Modern social theory associates the macrosocial with national society and the microsocial with the local level. With the intensification of the process of globalisation, the macrosocial has extended to encompass global society while the microsocial remains associated with the local level. However the microsocial is deeply influenced by the macrosocial so that it is also globalised to varying degrees. An example is the pre-eminence associated with some cities because of the transnational character of their political, economic and socio-cultural links: New York, Los Angeles, Tokyo, London, Paris.

Fourth, there is a partial erosion of the Nation-State as the regulating center of social life and identity-definer/builder. At the same time, the complex asymmetrical interdependence between countries is increasing, sometimes reflected in the fragmentation of national societies (e.g. Yugoslavia).

Fifth, there is a partial erosion in national democratic systems because of the greater and more mobile financial power of market players, be they multi-national corporations, investment funds, currency speculators. This is reflected in an increasing discrepancy between the territorial national-based system of representation and the transnational social forces-based system.

Although the literature on globalisation focuses mainly on the economic dimension, I consider globalisation to be a multidimensional process characterised by twelve inter-related elements: military, economic, financial, communications, religious, interpersonal, scientific-technological, population and migration, environmental, epidemiological, criminal and political. Each of these elements is discussed below.

Military

The military dimension of globalisation was the first to be developed, beginning with the 1941 attack by Japan on the US fleet at Pearl Harbor. This represented the first time that war acquired a truly global scope, bearing in mind that the First World War was a Europe-based conflict. The apogee of the military dimension of globalisation was in the second half of the 1950s when the US and the former Soviet Union first attained the capability to destroy the planet using intercontinental missiles armed with nuclear warheads, the so-called mutually assured destruction. In both groups, the military establishment overlapped with economic and scientific interests, producing the scientific-industrial military complex. The period following the Cuban missile crisis in 1962 until the beginning of the Reagan administration in 1981 saw some progress in the use of confidence-building measures as a basis for agreements to limit the arms race. This lessened but did not remove the risk of nuclear war. From 1981 to 1984 there was a re-intensification of military globalisation as a result of a major increase in the military budgets of the superpowers, the development of first strike tactical weapons and the attempt by the US to develop a self-defense doctrine that envisaged winning a nuclear war. The coming to power of Gorbatchev in the Soviet Union in 1985 marked the beginning of a reduction in the process of military globalisation through unilateral cuts in military spending, the acceptance of *in locus* verification of military facilities, and, since 1991, a rationalisation of the ex-Soviet armed forces. A partial deactivation or re-targeting of intercontinental missiles has also occurred since 1993. A general trend has been a reduction in arms expenditure although Asia is the exception.

Economic

The globalisation of the economy expanded in the 1950s with the emergence of the first multinational corporations. By the 1980s, these corporations had become transnational in reach with operations and strategic partnerships that spanned the globe. Also in the 1980s several medium-sized enterprises became transnational in operation but not size. Economic productivity increased tremendously as a result of new technologies (e.g. computer hardware and software, robotics, new materials, biotechnology) and management innovations (e.g. total quality control, 'just-in-time' manufacturing). The increased role of knowledge-based service industries in economic activity has reduced the demand for low and medium-skilled labour, resulting in high unemployment in many countries and encouraging new thinking on labour policies and human resource management. At the same time, there is an emerging differentiation between those countries that are active participants in the process of economic globalisation and those that are becoming marginalised. Intensified competition among countries is creating stronger pressures for clear 'rules of the game' concerning trade and investment at the global and regional levels. This is reflected in the creation of the World Trade Organization in 1994 and the formation of regional economic blocs such as the European Single Market, NAFTA, APEC, MERCOSUR, etc.

Seven categories of countries can be distinguished according to economic and other factors:

- Developed: economies based on knowledge-intensive production and services, strong attractiveness to investors and a high level of governance and per capita income: OECD countries, Chinese Taipei, Singapore, Hong Kong (China) and Israel;

- Superpower: has the same features as the Developed economies but with military power of global reach: USA;

- Continental: countries with a very large territory and population, medium per capita income, some advanced sectors and important military power: Russia, China, India and Brazil. Russia and China fulfill all the criteria of continental countries. India meets all the criteria except for per capita income, which is very low. Similarly, Brazil satisfies all criteria except military power, which is rated moderate. Brazil and China can also be considered as emerging countries.

- Emerging: countries with economic dynamism (or prospects therefor), medium per capita income and good medium-term potential for investors: Thailand, Malaysia, Indonesia, Philippines, Brunei, South Africa, Turkey, Hungary, Poland, Slovenia, Baltic States, Saudi Arabia, Kuwait, United Arab Emirates, Mexico, Costa Rica, Trinidad and Tobago, Chile, Argentina;

- Stagnant: countries with low economic dynamism, low or medium income per capita and low attractiveness to investors: Yugoslavia, Ukraine, Armenia, Burma, Jordan, Syria, Lebanon, Egypt, Peru, Ecuador, Bolivia, Paraguay, Kenya, Ghana;

- Extremely Poor: countries with no economic dynamism, low per capita income, unattractive to investors and precarious governance: large part of Africa, Bangladesh, Haiti; and

- Politically Excluded: countries in a state of civil war and/or non-government and/or governed according to extremely authoritarian rule or religious fundamentalism and/or terrorist states: Iraq, Iran, Afghanistan, North Korea.

Financial

This refers to the growth and geographical spread of capital markets, and in particular the growing role of electronic commerce. The diversity of financial products and the speed at which financial transactions occur pose important challenges for regulatory authorities. A diverse range of actors participate in the financial markets, including international financial institutions such as the World Bank, private banks and finance houses, pension funds, investment funds and even municipal authorities. The volatility of speculative money flows is a concern for the stability and predictability of the global financial system.

Communications

The globalisation of communications accelerated in the 1960s, encapsulated well by Marshall MacLuhan's reference to the "global village" and his phrase "the medium is the message". Beginning in the 1980s, the role of information technologies in our professional and personal lives has increased significantly especially in the areas of telecommunications, the internet and e-mail, cable television, etc. A growing minority of the world's population has the opportunity to travel to other countries, to learn and use different languages and to experience other cultures. Through television, the majority of the world's population has access to information about other societies. The globalisation of culture is far from homogeneous; on the contrary, there is strong emphasis in some countries on reaffirming differences and individuality through media such as films, music and literature.

Religious

The religious dimension of globalisation is one of the most complex because it is one with a long history: the principal religions of the world have been trans-civilization, trans-cultural and trans-national over the past two thousand years. However, in the past two decades there has been a new wave of expansion-contraction between the classic and emerging religions. This is characterized by the different positions they hold regarding the other dimensions of the globalisation process, especially the economic, financial and communications elements. Some religions support the process of globalisation (e.g. mainstream Protestantism, Catholicism and Judaism) while others oppose it (e.g. Islam, Hinduism, Orthodox-Oriental Christians, Liberation Theology Catholics, conservative Protestants, fundamentalist Judaism and fundamental Xintoism). Yet other religions seek to appeal to particular groups within society without necessarily supporting or opposing globalisation, e.g. Zen-Buddhism, Kardecist Spiritists and "New Ageists". Although different religions hold different views regarding globalisation, there is also support for ecumenicalism on certain issues such as environmental protection, prohibition of illegal drugs and hyper-consumption. New information technologies provide religious groups (and others) with the power to reach and influence a global audience of existing and potentially new members.

Interpersonal

This refers to the emergence and expansion of new forms of professional and personal relationships. Characteristics include self-reflexivity, greater support for multi-culturalism and multi-lingualism, a tendency to the androgynous, high geographical mobility and the development of the seven dimensions of intelligence, i.e. verbal, logic-mathematics, intra-personal, inter-personal, spatial, kinesics and musical. The interpersonal dimension is decisive to an understanding of the emergence of two new forms of relationships: that of man-woman-organization and woman-man-planetary. The first relationship concerns self-knowledge centred on strategic interaction and the individual's ego. The second focuses on self-knowledge oriented to both strategic and emotional interactions and collective responsibility.

Scientific-Technological

The scientific-technological dimension reflects the exponential increase in the interactions within and between specialised communities such the scientific, financial, medical, etc. through journals, video-conferencing, e-mail, the internet and workshops/conferences. The role of scientific inputs to decision-making processes has also increased -- within corporations, in inter-governmental organisations, in NGOs. National and international co-operation among institutions involved in teaching and research and corporate R&D departments is strengthening, boosting the efficiency of resource use and encouraging faster development of new products.

Population and Migration

The world's population is increasing at about 1.8% annually, adding almost 100 million inhabitants each year. This growth is spread very unevenly, creating critical situations in regions where the resources-population relationship is strained and/or where institutional efficiency is low, e.g. Africa, Middle East, South Asia and Central America. Controlling illegal migration has become an important policy issue with the efficacity of border controls in some countries coming under growing scrutiny. In this context, borders can be differentiated according to three types:

- entry subject to minimal constraints, such as for diplomats, those who are highly qualified and senior executives who move countries regularly as part of their careers;

- entry subject to satisfying all relevant controls, which applies to the vast majority of people travelling for personal or professional reasons. Controls include requirements to have a valid visa that defines the maximum length of stay and/or a return ticket and/or proof of adequate financial resources;

- entry prohibited for specific reasons.

Environmental

The globalisation of environmental problems such as ozone layer depletion, climate change and loss of biodiversity first came to the fore in the mid-1980s and catalysed collaborative work between physical scientists and social scientists as reflected, for example, in the research of the "Global Environmental Change" community. The Rio "Earth Summit" in 1992 and its emphasis on sustainable development resulted in political commitment to address global and national environmental problems through implementation of Agenda 21 and various multi-lateral environmental agreements. Meetings of the parties to these agreements have subsequently resulted in greater specificity in commitments. A key challenge in addressing environmental problems is to avoid, on the one hand, a belief that technology will always provide a solution, and, on the other hand, a New Romantic view that focuses only on changing consumption patterns and life-styles to the exclusion of scientific and technological innovation.

Epidemiological

This reflects the greater circulation of people through international travel, intensified use of medical products and increased contact with isolated communities. Such actions increase the potential for spreading harmful micro-organisms or bacterial resistance to antibiotics, which increases the vulnerability of humans to a pandemic. For example, the possible emergence of an air-transmitted lethal virus is a major concern to specialists in epidemiology and public health.

Criminal

International organized crime, which during the 1980s was centered on the drug-trafficking activities of Colombian and southwest Asian groups, has since been growing rapidly in other regions, e.g. Russia. Moreover, the goods in question now include advanced military equipment and radioactive material. Co-ordination among national police forces in combatting organised crime lags further and further behind for many reasons, e.g. lack of physical and financial resources, more sophisticated techniques being used by criminals and the erosive effect of bribery and corruption. In the mid-1990s, international organized crime represented approximately 3% of the world's GNP, growing at a rate of 15% a year. Techniques for laundering money back into the legal economy had become very sophisticated in some cases. International terrorism remains a threat although it has suffered important setbacks in the last decade. New forms of transnational terrorism associated with religious extremism are emerging and present important challenges to state and citizen security.

Political

The globalisation of politics rests on the advance of market and democratic systems over planned and authoritarian approaches. In the last decade, democratic or semi-democratic systems have been replacing authoritarian regimes in most countries of the world. Respect for human rights and open, multi-party elections have become more established in national political systems, although it is not uncommon to observe a significant gap between the rhetoric and the reality. Increased levels of education and higher incomes among voters is encouraging greater calls for government that is transparent in operation, accountable for performance and responsive to key social and economic issues. This is also reflected in the growth of NGOs and other types of citizens organisations, many of which are part of larger international networks.

As part of the political dimension, global governance in a range of areas rests on inter-governmental organisations such as the United Nations system, the International Monetary Fund, the World Bank, the WTO. In the 1990s, global governance is lagging behind the other dimensions of globalisation because of:

- conflict between the oligarchic (promoted by the G7 and the majority of developed countries) and democratic governance arrangements (promoted by the majority of medium-income and some low-income countries);

- lack of political leadership focused on the long term;

- the United Nations blocks the emergence of a new transnational governance system. For example, this could be instituted by having a General Assembly based on some type of proportional representation of world population and economic power: approximately 200 representatives of the world's population (independent of countries), 100 representatives of the countries, 200 representatives of multi-national corporations and 100 representatives of federations of the scientific and NGO communities. A Global Security Council formed by 30 members selected from the 600 representatives could have delegated responsibility for taking urgent decisions.

3.0 The Expansion of Environmentalism and the Formation of New Transnational Social Forces

National concern about environmental problems has been intensifying since the mid-1960s when the "environmental revolution" gained force in the US, catalysed by public reaction to books such as Rachel Carson's "Silent Spring". In the 1970s concern about environmental issues spread throughout Canada, Western Europe, Japan, New Zealand and Australia and in the 1980s it embraced Latin America, central and eastern Europe, the former Soviet Union and East and South Asia. The work of the Brundtland Commission and its report "Our Common Future" in the mid 1980s raised the profile of the environment and the concept of sustainable development. In the 1990s, as a result of the preparatory process leading up to the Rio "Earth Summit", an increased number of countries began to examine and debate seriously environmental issues. This included China and countries in Africa and the Middle East. The evolution of national consciousness-raising concerning the environment has been one of an upward curve with short plateau periods followed by a renewed rise in the curve.

As a consequence of three decades of national concern about environmental deterioration there has been an emergence and consolidation of:

- NGOs and grass-root environmental and public interest groups;

- national and sub-national environmental agencies responsible for environmental policy and conservation. In 1970 there were twelve national environmental agencies world-wide whereas by 1995 this had grown to more then 180;

- environmental science institutions and specific research communities, e.g. the "Global Environmental Change" scientific community in the USA;

- environmental specialists drawn from a wide range of academic disciplines;

- "green" consumerism, reflected in demands for organically-grown food, non-fossil fuel powered automobiles, energy-efficient appliances, recycled paper, reusable containers, products produced using clean technologies and raw materials produced in a sustainable manner;

- public information schemes that certify the environmental characteristics of products and their production, e.g. ecolabelling schemes, EMAS and ISO 14000;

- intergovernmental organisations and international agreements on the environment, such as the United Nations Environmental Program, the Vienna Convention and Montreal Protocol on substances that deplete the ozone layer, the Basel Convention on the control of transboundary movements of hazardous wastes and their disposal, and the conventions on climate change and biodiversity.

All the actors and processes identified above constitute the global environmental movement whose values and ideas are disseminated through a wide range of stakeholders inside and outside government. Environmentalism, which emerged as a movement involving a small number of people, groups and associations, has now been transformed into a transnational, multi-sectorial issue.

The development of environmentalism as a transnational phenomenon highlighted the differences in international politics at the beginning of the 1990s. These differences cluster around three groupings:

- those whose interest and orientation focus on the Nation-State (nationalists) versus those who emphasise the world scale (globalists);

- those who consider environmental protection of fundamental importance and inseparable from economic development (sustainabilists) versus those in favour of economic development separate from considerations of environmental protection (predatorians); and

- those in favour of a gradual redistribution of income nationally and internationally (progressives) versus those with a conservative social welfare perspective (conservatives).

The combination of these three groupings enables us to identify eight permutations in the world system: conservative-nationalists (CN), progressive-nationalists (PN), conservative-nationalist-sustainabilists (CNS), progressive-nationalist-sustainabilists (PNS), conservative-globalists (CG), progressive-globalists (PG), conservative-globalist-sustainabilists (CGS) and progressive-globalist-sustainabilists (PGS). Clearly, what follows is a generalisation and there will be exceptions in specific cases but the purpose here is to provide an organising taxonomy.

Conservative-nationalists support the establishment of protectionist economies and powerful armed forces, consider the Nation-State a superior entity to the international system, oppose growth in the power of the UN and fear the actions of transnational corporations. They are frequently racists. Examples of this type of grouping include the Republican far right and right wing militias (USA), the National Front (France), the National Alliance (Italy), regional oligarchies representing low productivity sectors (Brazil and Argentina) and the PRI right-wing (Mexico).

Progressive-nationalists favour the creation of protectionist economies with strong state intervention in the area of social justice, the maintenance of powerful armed forces, oppose the spread of transnational corporations and expansion of the UN's power. Examples include the left wing of the Workers Party in Brazil, the Communist Party in Chile, the Zapatista Front and the Revolutionary Democratic Party left wing in Mexico and sectors of the French Communist Party.

Conservative-nationalist-sustainabilists support national environmental protection, they reject the UN, oppose transnational corporations and favour the maintenance of powerful armed forces. The neo-Nazi sector in Germany and Austria, and fundamentalist sectors from Hinduism, Islam and Christianity are examples.

Progressive-nationalist-sustainabilists endorse sustainable development on a national scale and favour strong State intervention to promote social justice. They do not support the activities of the UN nor those of transnational corporations. Examples include large parts of the Workers Party in Brazil, sectors of the Chilean Communist Party and the Uruguayan Ample Front, parts of the French, Chilean and Brazilian Green Party, and elements of the French and Italian Communist Parties.

Conservative-globalists favour open market economies, a central role for transnational corporations, partial disarmament, a gradual enhancement of the UN's role and functions through partial limitation of the Nation-State's power in order to build a transnational authority based on a stratified structure of countries. This group also supports empowerment of an enlarged Security Council, and intergovernmental organisations such as the International Monetary Fund, the World Bank and the World Trade Organization. The Conservative-Globalists are the dominant force in the world political system and represent what is known as neoliberalism. Examples include large sections of the established North American, West European and Japanese political parties, the modernist parts of the Brazilian center and right parties, the Chilean National Party and the modernist sector of the Argentinean Justice Party.

Progressive-globalists support open market economies, a central role for transnational corporations, strong disarmament measures and a rapid development of global governance institutions, particularly to control the circulation of speculative capital. The left wing of liberal western parties such as the US Democratic Party, the French Socialists, the German Social-Democrats, the British Labour Party, and the Brazilian Social Democrats and the Chilean Socialist Party are examples.

Conservative-globalist-sustainabilists also favour open market economies and a central role for transnational corporations but support only partial disarmament. This group considers expeditious development of global governance institutions in the environment field as particularly important. Examples include sectors of the Dutch and Scandinavian Social-Democrat Parties and the French Generation Ecologique Party.

Progressive-globalist-sustainabilists consider that the waste-intensive and energy-inefficient lifestyle which predominates in high and medium-income countries is morally and economically wrong. This group supports deep reform of the international order and a central role for environmental policies in domestic politics. In addition, they endorse the concept of ecologically sustainable development and the reduction of social inequalities locally and globally. Addressing these inequalities should be achieved by fostering the integration of presently marginalised countries into the world economy and through subsidised transfer by the rich countries of environmentally-sound technologies. This group is in favor of the immediate establishment of a supranational authority, combining the transnational and international, to deal with global social and environmental issues. Although from a normative point of view they support the democratic approach to global governance, this group is willing to accept oligarchic forms provided that it accelerates the overall process. Parts of the Dutch, Scandinavian and Brazilian Social-Democrat left wing, and the German, Austrian, Scandinavian, French, Brazilian and Chilean Green Parties are examples of this group's supporters.

The Nation-State's regulatory capabilities are weakened by the process of globalisation, in particular its economic, financial and communications dimensions. In some cases, this is further affected by deficiencies in, or the breakdown of, domestic socio-political structures concerning, *inter alia*, governance and democracy. The extreme outcome is separatism and national disintegration.

We are beginning to observe a split between those in society who are active participants in the global economy and those who are becoming excluded. The extent of this split varies widely from country to country, and even among different regions in a country. For illustrative purposes, the following is my personal estimation of the degree of individuals' participation (i.e. inclusion) in the global economy: almost 100% in Singapore, Japan and Norway; 90% in the European Union member states; 80% in the USA, Korea and Kuwait; 60% in Chile, Costa Rica and Malaysia; 40% in Thailand, Brazil, Argentina and Mexico; 10% in Peru, Bolivia, Nicaragua and Nigeria; and less than 5% in Haiti, Zaire and Sudan.

Globalisation is also changing social dynamics through:

- technological developments, especially the rising demand for skilled labour and the increased role of information technologies in all types of economic activity. This has flow-on implications for employment/unemployment patterns;

- migration and population growth, and the pressures this places on social integration and access to scarce environmental resources;

- socio-cultural attitudes and habits, especially the balance between individual and collective responsibility and the materialistic consumption patterns characteristic of modern societies;

- politics, especially the focus on the short-term rather than the long-term in decision-making. Contributory factors include the short electoral cycles against which politicians' performance is measured and the influence of special interest groups in lobbying for their position.

4.0 Global Environmental Governance: Progress and Impasse

Arrangements for global environmental governance, principally institutions and international agreements, have been developing quickly, although not necessarily coherently. Seven achievements over the last decade stand out:

- the promulgation of the Vienna Convention (1985), the Montreal Protocol (1987) and the London Amendment (1990) concerning protection of the ozone layer;

- the creation in 1991, and subsequent consolidation, of the Global Environment Facility to fund projects covering control of pollution of international waters, responding to climate change and ozone layer depletion, and protection of biodiversity;

- the 1991 Madrid Protocol to the 1959 Antarctic Treaty which postpones for fifty years development of Antarctica's natural resources;

- the endorsement by heads of state of Agenda 21 at the 1992 Rio "Earth Summit", providing the global 'blueprint' for implementing sustainable development;

- the signature and entry into force of the 1992 UN Framework Convention on Climate Change;

- the signature and entry into force of the 1992 Convention on Biodiversity; and

- the establishment in 1993 of the UN Commission for Sustainable Development.

Protection of the Ozone Layer: The Montreal Protocol

The Montreal Protocol is the best example of success in building international regimes for protecting the global environment. The use and production of CFCs has fallen dramatically in developed countries since the beginning of the 1990s and has been closely controlled in other countries although illegal trade in CFCs does remain a problem. Four factors underpin the overall successful result: the rapid achievement of consensus in the scientific community about the severity of the problem and the efficiency of information exchange within this community, the fact that CFC production is concentrated among a few key players in the private sector, focused leadership by one country in the international negotiations and the fast response by CFC producers in investing in the research and development of alternative technologies that were commercially feasible.

The Global Environment Facility

The operation of the Facility is being slowly consolidated and it has become an efficient mechanism for transferring multilateral resources for specific projects. Although the amount of resources available for disbursement is small compared to needs, the achievements to date have been commendable. Several features have contributed to the success of the Facility's work: a negotiation process in which the developed countries endorsed a democratic decision-making process and developing countries took seriously the need to achieve efficiency in the Facility's operations, the formation of a dynamic *ad hoc* structure to manage funds involving the UNDP, UNEP and the World Bank, and a multi-disciplinary approach to problem analysis and project implementation.

The Madrid Protocol to the Antarctic Treaty

For some time leading up to negotiation of the Protocol, Parties to the Antarctic Treaty had been examining intensively the implications of opening up Antarctica to minerals development. At the Madrid conference of the parties a coalition led by Australia, France and international NGOs (particularly Greenpeace) managed to secure a 50 year deferment of minerals exploitation on the continent. This outcome meant that the debate between preservationists (who propose that Antarctica be an international park from which all economic activities are permanently banned) and conservationists (who support a judicious development of some of Antarctica's mineral resources) swung significantly in favour of the former.

Agenda 21

Agenda 21, agreed at Rio, has been a relatively effective programme for promoting sustainable development. After the Rio "Earth Summit" some countries elaborated national Agenda 21s, the provisions of which were reflected to varying degrees in some national planning strategies, e.g. China. Several organs of the UN system redefined or reoriented their programmes to support implementation of sustainable development, e.g. UNDP. In spite of the positive impacts of Agenda 21, a decrease in the profile of environmental issues among the public post-Rio and a decline in interest in building "institutions for the earth" has meant that the document has not been as important in mobilising and sustaining commitments as its supporters envisaged. In this context, the expectation is that the Programme for the Further Implementation of Agenda 21, agreed at UNGASS in June 1997, will re-invigorate efforts.

UN Framework Convention on Climate Change

To date, the climate change convention has been a failure because of:

- weak leadership by major greenhouse gas emitting countries and limited progress in meeting stabilisation targets;

- reluctance on the part of developing countries to commit to specific reduction targets;

- disagreement among the scientific and economic community about respectively, the pace and extent of climate change, and the costs and benefits of alternative response strategies.

Nonetheless, at the Kyoto Conference of the Parties in December 1997 there was some progress with the agreement of a Protocol. A key challenge now is to ensure ratification and implementation of the Protocol as well as to increase co-operation with developing countries in preparing national response policies and measures.

Biodiversity Convention

This Convention has had a double impact. On the one hand, it has significantly increased international public awareness about the importance of biological diversity, an area not well known outside a specialist community before the 1990s, and it also introduced the concept of "common concern of humankind." On the other hand, its implementation has been constrained by the attitude of the US concerning the Convention's provisions for the protection of intellectual property rights. This is particularly significant given that two-thirds of the world's scientific and technological capacity in biodiversity research and biotechnology is located in the US. Efforts to protect biodiversity and to promote its sustainable development are extremely diverse and not always encouraging. For example, while countries such as Costa Rica and Belize have established agreements for pharmacological and alimentary research with transnational corporations, others such as Brazil, Malaysia and Mexico still lack effective policies for biodiversity protection.

UN Commission for Sustainable Development

The United Nations Commission for Sustainable Development (UN CSD), established in 1993 after its creation by the General Assembly in 1992, has developed slowly and has to date had questionable influence in international relations. The destiny of the UN CSD was connected to the obsolescence of the main bodies of the UN (especially the General Assembly and ECOSOC) and to the failure of reformist efforts that seemed to hold promise when Butros Butros Ghali was appointed Secretary-General of the UN in January 1992. The UN Commission on Global Governance lead by Kenneth Carlson that produced the 1995 report "Our Global Neighborhood", and the Commission on the Fiftieth Anniversary of the UN, led by Paul Kennedy, were excellent initiatives and presented innovative proposals for reforming the UN. Unfortunately, their impact on the organization has been minimal.

Impasse: Mainstreaming the Environment in the UN System

At the time of the Rio "Earth Summit" optimists envisioned that environmental issues would drive the UN and be the principal catalyst for internal structural reform. What actually happened was the contrary: the inefficiency and the inertia of the UN system obstructed the dynamism of environmental issues. Today, it is evident that a mainstreaming of environmental issues into the UN system depends on deep structural reform within the organisation, which may require shifting from an international-intergovernmental system to a transnational-transgovernmental system.

In the absence of strong actors to champion change, however, "business-as-usual" prevails. Countries such as the US, France, the UK, Russia, China, India, Brazil, Korea and Indonesia oppose strongly any shift to a transnational-transgovernmental system. Others such as Germany, Italy and Canada are reticent while Japan, the Netherlands and Sweden are mildly favorable. Many representatives of transnational corporations oppose the idea because of perceptions about increased controls on their global operations, while international NGO's are generally in favour. The position of the scientific community is unclear and that of major religious groups is ambiguous. In this environment, any changes are likely to be incremental.

REFERENCES

BROWN, L. R. et al., 1995 and 1996: *State of the World. A Worldwatch Institute Report on Progress Toward a Sustainable Society.* W.W. Norton and Co. New York.

BUZAN, B., 1991: *People, States and Fear. An Agenda for International Security Studies in the Post-Cold War Era.* Harvester Wheatsheaf. London.

CAIRNCROSS, F., 1992: *Costing the Earth. The Challenge for Governments, the Opportunities for Business.* Harvard Business School Press.

CALDWELL, L.J., 1990: *Between Two Worlds. Science, the Environmental Movement and Policy Choice.* Cambridge University Press.

COMMISSION ON GLOBAL GOVERNANCE , 1995: *Our Global Neighborhood.* Oxford University Press.

FOSSAERT, R., 1991: *Le Monde au 21ème Siècle. Une théorie des systèmes mondiaux.* Fayard. Paris.

GUIDENS, A., 1990: *The Consequences of Modernity*. Cambridge University Press.

HELD, D., 1995: *Democracy and the Global Order. From the Modern State to Cosmopolitan Governance*. Polity Press. Cambridge.

HURRELL, A. and KINGSBURY, B., 1992: *The International Politics of the Environment*. Clarendon Press. Oxford.

KENNEDY, P., 1993: *Preparing for the Twenty-First Century*. Random House. New York.

MACNEILL, J., WINSEMIUS, P. and YAKUSHIJI, T., 1991: *Beyond Interdependence. The Merging of The World's Economy and the Earth's Ecology*. Oxford University Press. New York.

MORIN, E. et KERN, A., 1993: *Terre-Patrie*. Seuil. Paris.

NORTH, R., 1990: *War, Peace, Survival. Global Politics and Conceptual Synthesis*. Westview Press. Boulder.

PORTER, G. and BROWN, J., 1991: *Global Environmental Politics*. Westview Press. Boulder.

RISSE-KAPPEN, T. (ed.), 1995: *Bringing Transnational Relations Back In. Non-State Actors, Domestic Structures and International Institutions*. Cambridge University Press.

ROSENAU, J., 1990: *Turbulence in World Politics. A Theory of Change and Continuity*. Princeton University Press.

SAND, P., 1990: *Lessons Learned in Global Environmental Governance*. World Resources Institute. Washington D.C.

STERN, P., YOUNG, O. and DRUCKMAN, D. (eds), 1992: *Global Environmental Change. Understanding the Human Dimensions*. National Academy Press. Washington D.C.

WERKSMAN, J., 1996: *Greening International Institutions*. Earthscan Publications. London.

ZOLO, D., 1995: *Cosmopolis. La prospettiva del Governo Mondiale*. Feltrinelli. Milan.

FREE TRADE AND THE GLOBAL ENVIRONMENT AS INTERNATIONAL PUBLIC GOODS

Djamester Simarmata
Centre for Policy and Implementation Studies, Indonesia

1.0 Introduction

Two types of globalisation can be identified. First, economic globalisation associated with international trade and investment and the communications revolution. Second, globalisation of environmental issues. The two are inter-connected. Economic globalisation involves not only trade in goods such as automobiles, wood products, steel, petrochemicals, etc. but also trade in services covering, for example, telecommunications, banking and insurance and consulting. The globalisation of environmental issues is growing through, for example, international efforts to address global-warming as a side-effect of increased economic activities.

Production processes and the consumption of goods and services generate wastes which are emitted or discharged into the environment, adding to the level of pollutant stocks. Some of these stocks appear close to the threshold level where the absorption capacity of the environment is exceeded. The negative environmental impacts of greenhouse gas emissions are perhaps the most well publicised, whether in a regional or global context. The experience of Southeast Asian countries in late 1997 concerning air pollution from forestry fires in Indonesia is an example of a regional issue with important transboundary economic and environmental impacts.

Trade theory tells us that international trade will promote specialisation, which will increase productivity. The father of modern economics Adam Smith noted this relationship more than two hundreds years ago. At that time, the availability of natural resources seemed limitless and the environment was considered a free good. Both of these perceptions were closely linked to the prevailing population level and degree of economic activity. Two hundred years ago, the earth's population was less than 1 billion; in 1996 it was more than 5 billion. In 1996, the total world output value at market exchange rates stood at nearly US$30 trillion. Today's high population and the multiplication of real incomes has opened up a new consumption frontier, which in turn poses a new challenge to the environment.

The distribution of total world income is highly uneven, with the share attributed to the industrialised countries being substantially higher than that of developing countries. Economic globalisation provides a means for developing countries to participate more fully in international trade, and hence to increase their share of total world income. Similarly, growing private capital flows between developed and developing countries enhance the rate of foreign investment in the latter, especially in natural resource industries. This is encouraging, but at the same time it raises new issues at the economy-environment interface.

The rate of economic growth is much higher for the developing countries, in part because of the process of globalisation. Technology transfer through international trade is an integral element of enhancing economic growth through improving resource efficiencies and productivity. "Leap-frogging" to cleaner, more efficient technologies is only made possible by freer international trade. Nonetheless, it appears that although the highest absolute levels of pollution associated with production and consumption are in the industrialized countries, the rate of growth in pollution is much higher in the developing countries.

2.0 Free Trade As An International Public Good

The notion that free trade can be regarded as an international public good stems from the potential welfare benefits to the international community. It has an analogy in the provision of a road to a community or country. The road is considered a public good with positive welfare benefits for society. In a similar manner, the more participants involved in free trade the higher the potential welfare benefits to all due to more intensive specialisation, leading to higher productivity. It should be recalled, however, that free trade necessitates the re-specialisation of countries consistent with their comparative advantages. Otherwise stated, free trade will promote a new pattern of trade which in turn will stimulate a restructuring of economic activities in participating countries. In the short-run, the restructuring process could result in considerable economic, environmental and social impacts.

The environmental impacts of restructuring could be both positive or negative, e.g. the adoption of cleaner production or eco-efficiency as an integral element of industrial restructuring could promote pollution prevention and waste minimisation; on the other hand, lack of reform of environmentally-damaging subsidies for raw materials or energy could exacerbate existing problems. Changes in the trade pattern between countries is likely to change the spatial location of production activities, which in turn will change relative pollution emission loadings. The environmental impacts of production activities can be at the local, national, regional or global levels and are not mutually exclusive.

Increased flows of investment and re-specialisation have catalysed greater industrial relocation. One of the most visible implications of this is the relocation of pollution-intensive industrial processes, frequently to less developed countries. Concern has been expressed about "pollution havens" and "technology dumping" but the empirical evidence is sparse. There are clearly some industries in some countries where examples can be found -- especially those industries that face higher than average pollution control costs -- but these appear to be the exceptions rather than the general rule. A recent report notes that most shifts in investment are related to structural adjustments rather than because of lower environmental standards[1]. It should also be recalled that in the investment decision analysis environmental regulations and standards are but one consideration among many. Other factors that are assessed include a country's economic and fiscal policies, its political stability, the availability, skill levels and costs of labour, and the availability and condition of infrastructure such as road networks and ports, etc.

---

[1]   OECD, 1997: *Economic Globalisation and the Environment*. OECD. Paris.

Globalisation increases opportunities for the outsourcing of components, with the potential for a particular country to specialise in one or more components of the final product. International trade now occurs not only in final or finished goods but also in semi-finished goods or product components. Usually the assembly of product components, which are usually of lower strategic value, more labour-intensive and may involve more pollution-intensive processes, is carried out in developing countries. Where domestic environmental policies and regulations are either inadequate or poorly enforced the increased scale effects of economic activities will tend to raise pollution levels in these countries.

Under the Polluter-Pays Principle "the sustainable and economically efficient management of environmental resources requires the internalisation of pollution prevention, control and damage costs"[2] (page 6). In international trade a problem arises as to the allocation of the relevant costs and how to reflect it in the final price of products. As previously noted, pollutants have different spatial impacts at local, regional and global levels while pollutant release occurs during the manufacture, use and final disposal of a product. The difficulty of the cost allocation problem is most evident at the local and/or regional level, and in particular identifying whether the relevant cost occurs during the manufacture, use or final disposal of a product. For example, in the case of products to be used domestically the relevant environmental costs should be reflected in the final price. Where the product is to be exported, the environmental costs during manufacture should not be charged to the final price but applied only up to the point of export. Such an approach could be considered as dumping, however.

The environmental costs associated with final disposal of a product, in the form of residual waste for example, could be very high. In the case of a used battery, this might be the mercury which remains. If the costs associated with product disposal had been included in the price, this should be excluded from the export price. The present system of product pricing does not reflect this, however. Pricing in relation to internalising environmental costs in traded goods requires further examination by both governments and the WTO.

3.0   Tropical Forests As An International Public Good

A particularly controversial issue concerns tropical forests, which are regarded as an important carbon "sink" for the absorption of CO_2 emissions. Countries with forests which act as carbon sinks provide environmental services for the benefit of humankind. However, this is not reflected in the valuation of, and potential mechanisms for compensating developing countries such as Indonesia and Brazil for, these services.

Because of the global public goods function of carbon sinks, the community of nations should contribute to the maintenance, enlargement and preservation of tropical forests. From the perspective of developing countries which are home to tropical forests, the preservation of these forests as carbon sinks has an opportunity cost because of the foregone income from exploitation. International interest in tropical forests should include not only awareness raising about their role as carbon sinks but also extend to practical assistance in tackling the roots of the problem, especially the economic aspects. By accepting or claiming that tropical forests have an international public goods function, the international community should contribute actively to the financing of tropical forests management.

---

[2]   OECD, 1992: The Polluter-Pays Principle. OECD General Distribution Document OCDE/GD(92)81. Environment Directorate, OECD. Paris.

Tropical forests are an important source of biodiversity. To protect biodiversity it may not be necessary to preserve an entire tropical forest, however. By preserving approximately 30% of a well selected, species-rich ecology in a tropical forest it may be possible to maintain a minimum core of biodiversity. This suggests that 70% of a tropical forest could be exploited without destroying its biodiversity role and with the possibility of enabling people living in the tropical forests to increase their welfare through a higher standard of living. In addition, the tropical forests will continue to carry out their CO_2 absorption function through the process of photosynthesis.

In a steady-state equilibrium the absorbed CO_2 would be offset by that released from dying trees or branches. This steady-state would be achieved if the forest were left untouched for its entire life. Preserving the entire tropical forest has been proposed by some commentators but as noted above there are opportunities to obtain multiple uses from tropical forests: protect biodiversity, establish a wood products market and provide a carbon sink to absorb CO_2 emissions. For the latter, an appropriate valuation of the environmental "service" provided by carbon absorption needs to be calculated. What is critical is a continuous rejuvenation of tropical forests. This is achievable through a robust, well enforced forest management policy that promotes sustainable development.

Wood harvested from tropical forests should be transformed into durable goods such as tables, chairs and other household goods and housing components. The idea is to have a lot of wood durable products, so that we can store the carbon in those products. This is analogous to the action of "storing" carbon in households. The more durable tropical wood products we have, the more we lock in CO_2. A balance is needed, however, since by using more tropical wood products we are removing CO_2 from the atmosphere and storing it. Instead of limiting trade in tropical wood products, we should encourage and expand it conditional upon the cutting of tropical forests in an ecologically sustainable manner. In this way, our environmental goals to control global warming by reducing CO_2 in the atmosphere could be achieved using market forces[3].

Some commentators have proposed that metal and aluminum might substitute for furniture or housing components made from tropical wood. However, in producing aluminum large amounts of electricity, which is often generated by the use of oil or coal, are required and for each ton of aluminum approximately 22 tons of CO_2 are emitted[4]. Instead of releasing CO_2 tropical wood products store it. Substituting metal for wood products from tropical forests sounds attractive but may ultimately be counterproductive in reducing levels of CO_2 in the atmosphere.

4.0   Carbon Taxes and Reforestation of Tropical Forests

The introduction of carbon taxes has been discussed at some length and some countries have implemented them, e.g. Sweden and the Netherlands. These taxes focus on reducing the use of fossil fuels, be it directly through a reduction in consumption or indirectly through promoting their more efficient use or the wider adoption of alternative fuels such as gas.

---

[3]   See my article on this subject in Far Eastern Economic Review: "Logging for Clean Air", 4 February, 1993, pg 28.

[4]   See Atkins, P.R. et al. in Tester, J.W et al., 1991: *Energy and the Environment in the 21st Century*. MIT Press. Cambridge, Massachusetts.

In an earlier section of the paper the international public goods function of tropical forests was discussed as well as the view that all countries should contribute to the financing of the environmental services provided by such forests in the form of carbon sinks. The funds should be used for extending planted forest areas. Those parts of the forest which are used for commercial plantation should not receive public funding. There should, however, be special efforts to fund research into ways to prolong the durability of tropical wood products. The present state-of-the-art in wood technology means that wood products will ultimately end up as waste, either being recycled in a number of ways or re-releasing carbon to the atmosphere. If a technology could be developed so that the durability of wood products were increased comparable to that of metal products then they would store carbon for longer. A recent development in this direction is the production of ceramics from wood in Japan. Some of the funds from carbon taxes in developed countries could be used to extend such research in addition to a direct contribution to developing countries for the environmental services provided by tropical forests as carbon sinks and sources of biodiversity.

Through the provision of such funds developed countries would then have a sounder basis for influencing the forest management policy in developing countries. In that context, a shared goal should be to ensure that CO_2 absorption programmes are delivered cost-effectively. This would also encourage the enlargement of forest areas in the tropical developing countries for the benefit of all. Tradable permits, offsets and bubbles in a global context are instruments meriting further examination. As an example, for each additional kilogram of CO_2 emitted, an equal amount of absorption capacity in a newly reforested area should be available.

5.0   Conclusions

Further elaboration is needed of which "services" provided by tropical forests are reflected in the market through, for example, trade; which have a purely public goods role; and which have a mixed role. The discussions should involve forest biology, environmental economics and international trade specialists. The objective would be to identify the true costs and benefits of each forest "service" from a global perspective. In this context, one idea that might be examined further concerns the principle of symmetrical treatment of externalities applied on the global scale.

SUSTAINABILITY IN AN ERA OF GLOBALISATION: THE BUSINESS RESPONSE

Bjorn Stigson
World Business Council for Sustainable Development, Switzerland

1.0   Introduction

The World Business Council for Sustainable Development (WBCSD) is a coalition of some 125 leading international companies and is at the forefront of the business response to the challenges arising from the 1992 Rio "Earth Summit".   It has become the pre-eminent business voice on sustainable development issues. Its members are drawn from 35 countries and more than 20 major industrial sectors, and represented in the Council by the chief executive officers. It also benefits from a strong global network of national and regional business councils and partner organizations.

From a business perspective, sustainable development is built on three pillars: economic growth, ecological balance and social progress.   Sustainable development is not a clear and easily defined objective, however.   In 1997, WBCSD launched a scenario project to define more precisely what sustainable development in a future world might mean for business[1].

Two parameters distinguish the scenarios. First, uncertainties regarding natural ecosystems or rather their resilience to change. Scientific knowledge of ecological thresholds is limited, and the consequences of this are twofold: we do not know how much time society has to make the transition to sustainability and how near are we to any critical limits of ecosystems that could mean sudden step changes in the way natural systems function; and the discount rate that should be given to projects to reflect the value of future outcomes in current prices.   With a discount rate of 8-10% outcomes occurring more than, say, 10 years in the future are valued close to zero in today's prices. The higher the uncertainty, the higher the discount rate and the shorter is the time horizon for expected returns on private (and sometimes public) investment.

Second, global governance. What kind of future world can we foresee? Will the trend towards the market economy continue and can we make markets function in a more sustainable way? Will regulations and standards be more dynamic and performance-oriented rather than prescriptive? Will we see a return to "big" government? Will existing or redefined international institutions be capable of steering development in a more sustainable direction?

---

[1]   For an overview see WBCSD, 1998: Exploring Sustainable Development: WBCSD Global Scenarios 2000-2050 Summary Brochure. WBCSD. Switzerland.

2.0   Business's Response to the Challenges of Sustainable Development

Since the Rio "Earth Summit" the business sector has made great progress in implementing sustainable development. The achievements are summarised in the WBCSD's 1997 report "Signals of Change: Business Progress Towards Sustainable Development". The report identifies a number of such "signals of change" -- changes in direction and in momentum towards sustainable development. Some signals are stronger than others and some signals are controversial in that they can be interpreted in different ways but a basic shift in emphasis among many leading businesses is discernible.

This shift is characterised as one of moving from considering environmental issues as peripheral to business to a holistic view of business and sustainable development. More specifically:

- moving from a focus on costs and threats to savings and opportunities;

- shifting from end-of-pipe pollution clean-up to pollution prevention through cleaner production and waste minimisation;

- replacing linear "through-put" process methods with integrated systems approaches that emphasise materials recycling and re-use;

- viewing environmental and social issues as responsibilities not just for experts but for managers and employees throughout the enterprise;

- moving from confidentiality to greater transparency and accountability; and

- strengthening dialogue with a wider range of stakeholders: government, trade unions, NGOs, consumer groups, etc.

3.0   Drivers to the Business Response

The business response to sustainable development has gone through three phases. In the first phase, the focus was on "end-of-pipe" clean-up measures driven by the demands of regulation and public pressure to address threats to public health from air, soil and water pollution. The second phase, occurring in recent years, has focused on the concept of eco-efficiency, in which "win-win" benefits are obtained through improved financial and environmental performance.   In the third phase, which some leading companies have entered, environmental performance is being integrated into corporate strategic planning as a factor of competitive advantage. The following quotes illustrate this view:

"During the next quarter century, the most significant net contribution to a greener world will be made by industry...Not every company is there yet but most are trying. Those that aren't trying won't be a problem simply because they won't be around long term."

Ed Woolard, former Chairman, DuPont Chemicals.

"Environment will represent one of the biggest possibilities for technical and leadership-based innovation - and profitable companies - which the world has ever witnessed".

Percy Barnevik, Chief Executive Officer, ABB.

4.0 The Role of An Enabling Policy Framework

If we want society and business to move towards sustainability it is not sufficient to just concentrate on the operations of business. There is also a need for governments to establish an enabling policy framework. In this context, the "Signals of Change" report identified some of the key elements which the business sector considers important:

- sustained commitment to the principle of free trade and open market access;

- stable and predictable 'rules of the game' that provide for a level playing field between domestic and foreign businesses;

- realistic and enforceable target-setting;

- strengthened consultation with all stakeholders in civil society to build consensus on responsibilities to implement national and international environmental goals;

- removal of tariff and non-tariff barriers to the transfer of cleaner technologies;

- stronger efforts to improve the environmental awareness of consumers;

- implementation of economic instruments that motivate behaviour modification; and

- wider use of voluntary agreements and other self-regulatory approaches.

5.0 Environmental Performance and Shareholder Value

Despite the economic and environmental benefits accruing from eco-efficiency, in the absence of performance measures of progress towards sustainability the pace of transition by the business sector will be slower than might be expected. This reflects a view that 'what you cannot measure, you cannot manage'. Eco-efficiency needs to be reflected in shareholder value and eco-efficient companies need to be recognized by the financial markets. In this context, much remains to be done. A 1997 WBCSD report entitled "Environmental Performance and Shareholder Value", co-authored by representatives from DuPont, Swiss Bank Corporation and Storebrand, concluded that:

- to date, financial markets have generally recognised only negative environmental performance rather than viewing good environmental performance as a 'plus';

- good environmental performance can enhance the competitive advantage of a company;

61

- environmental issues and financial performance are linked;

- the quality of a company's environmental management is a good indicator of the overall quality of its business management; and

- the evaluation of environmental factors in the financial marketplace has been hindered by the absence of a financially relevant analytical framework.

These findings suggest that corporate environmental reporting and improving the environmental awareness of financial market actors (banks, insurers, credit rating agencies, etc.) are important opportunities to influence attitudinal changes.

6.0   Business and Sustainability: Priority Issues

Business is now addressing a much broader agenda than previously, in which a number of emerging priorities can be identified. These include:

- corporate social responsibility. This relates to the evolving roles of companies in a globalising economy and changing expectations associated with business's "social license to operate". For example, many governments have increased the contestability of public goods and services provision by privatising or corporatising former monopolies, e.g. urban water services and transport, and through greater reliance on out-sourcing. This is stimulating new opportunities for public-private sector partnerships. It is also redefining responsibilities, e.g. balancing on the one hand profit and rate of return on investments, and, on the other hand, a social responsibility to provide equitable, affordable access to services by the community.

- sustainable consumption. Interest in promoting sustainable production and consumption patterns has strengthened since the 1992 Rio "Earth Summit" when it was first raised on the international agenda. The business sector has made strenuous efforts to improve production efficiencies and is committed to do more. Progress on the consumption side is much more difficult as it involves complicated, and controversial, economic and social trade-offs that go the heart of our lifestyles and material aspirations.

- "greening" national accounts and sustainable development indicators. Conventional measures of economic activity such as GDP or GNP do not take into account the depletion of natural resources and the reduction of environmental quality. In this context, much work has focused on defining and refining methodologies of environmental accounting ("green" GDP), although practical applications have been limited . As major users of natural resources, both renewable and non-renewable, business has an important role to play in providing data for such types of accounts[2]. The development and adoption of indicators of sustainable development is an urgent task to enable all stakeholders—

---

[2]   Many large businesses already undertake some form of environmental accounting to identify potential cost savings in materials inputs and processing. See for example, Yakowitz, H. 1997: "Assessing the Cost-effectiveness of Cleaner Production" in OECD, 1997: *Cleaner Production and Waste Minimisation in OECD and Dynamic Non-Member Economies.* OECD Proceedings Series. OECD. Paris.

government, business, trade unions, the general public, NGOs, etc.—to track progress in making the transition to sustainable development. The quantitative information provided by such indicators could stimulate a profound change in the ways in which companies manage their resource use.

- <u>Subsidies.</u> The World Resources Institute has estimated that subsidies in the world economy amount to US$1,000 billion annually, primarily to subsidise resource use. Reform of subsidies could promote both more efficient use of economic resources and environmental improvements by re-orienting signals about the "cost" of pollution and natural resource use.

7.0   Conclusion

The manner in which environmental factors impact on business is a growing concern for many companies today. For leading businesses, globalisation and the environment are increasingly seen as opportunities for enhancing competitive advantage.

The major environmental challenges that business has to face might be defined under three categories. First, the short-term risks of sudden events, such as accidental pollution spills, which can result in substantial remediation costs or fines and adversely affect a company's share price. The question of "how clean is clean enough, and at what cost?" is also important in this context.

Second, the medium-term risk of not reading market signals correctly and failing to redesign products and processes to meet consumer demands for more environmentally-friendly goods can lead to loss of market share.

Third, the longer-term risks associated with uncertainty about approaching the limits of ecosystem functioning. In view of this uncertainty, society demands that business adopt a precautionary approach to global environmental issues such as ozone depletion or climate change. A major challenge for business is: "How much should we to invest today to minimise the consequences of future global environmental change?" This third category of risks places business in a very difficult dilemma concerning the discharge of their corporate and social responsibilities. A scenario approach provides one way to examine options and strategic responses.

SUSTAINABILITY CHALLENGES IN THE INFORMATION AGE

Jih Chang Yang
Industrial Technology Research Institute, Chinese Taipei

1.0   Introduction

The world is moving into the information age. It will be an age of extraordinary technical and social change, with unprecedented challenges to -- and opportunities for -- implementing sustainable development.

Interestingly, the most significant factor not being given nearly the attention it deserves in sustainability deliberations is the arrival of the information age. It packs such power, promises such sweeping changes and is so recognized for its dominant role in shaping our future that it is surprising why it has been so peripheral to the sustainable development debate.

For example, consider the raw power of information technology and how the pace of change is accelerating. In the next 15 years, new developments in information technology are likely to be momentous. The processing power of semiconductors is expected to grow by 2 to 3 orders of magnitude (Figure 1). This is the so-called Moore's Law. While it represents the single most breathtaking technical advance, the speed represented by Moore's Law is now being eclipsed by the growth of transmission power. A combination of the expansion in usable bandwidth and digital signal compression will increase the transmission rate of "bits" by 5 to 6 orders of magnitude in the next 15 years. The electronics at our fingertips will then be able to process the "bits" about a thousand times faster still, making the combined information power 100 million to a billion times greater in the next 15 years, or an increase of approximately 10 times every two years (Figure 2).

What will truly transform our lives, however, will be the so-called "connection power". Currently there are about 200 million computers which are being connected together through the Internet and other networks. By 2005 the number of computers in use is expected to grow to about 500 million. Considering that mathematicians have established that the "intelligence" of a network is proportional to the square of the number of its constituent members, the popular phrase "only connect" takes on a whole new meaning. In addition, non-computer chips, which are found in all kinds of products and equipment, totalling 6 billion today and growing faster than computer processors, are also being increasingly interconnected through wired or wireless means. One can well imagine what a very "smart" and "organic" whole our world could become when so much information power is connected together.

What would so much information power mean? Arguably, with major improvements in efficiency, productivity and value creation in the coming decades, our economies could undergo a profound transformation into something called the "Network Economy".

In the Network Economy, value migrates inexorably to the Network, and "networking" becomes a competitive imperative. Everybody feeds the Network for ways to get ahead while taking care to build specialisation in "core competencies". Efficiency will improve, costs will fall. Wealth flows from innovation for the unknown, not optimisation of the known. There will be perpetual disruptions as the turnover rate shortens: replacement and substitution may become so rapid that products will be released and phased out concurrently. Networking power will further concentrate innovation potential with the "haves". Silicon Valley's dominance in information technology, for example, will grow. The division of labour among companies and nations will deepen. Everybody will be racing to build and fortify their specific niches. Product life cycles will further shorten. Life cycle environmental responsibilities will become more complex with multiple stakeholders having a vested interest in "cradle to grave" and extended producer responsibility strategies. All of these changes will impact upon the process of economic globalisation.

2.0   Sustainability in the Information Age

What are the implications of so much information power for sustainability? Consider what it would take to reach sustainability.

Sustainable development is based on the integration of economic and environmental goals as a coherent and mutually reinforcing system. In real and practical terms, the challenge for sustainable development is *"To promote economic growth while simultaneously minimising the negative environmental impacts of that growth."*

How are we to achieve that? The answer is *"We need to dematerialise as fast as we grow."*

Here the word "dematerialise" denotes measures that reduce the content of energy, natural resources and raw materials in each unit of economic output. The logic is straightforward. If our economy is to grow at, say, 3 percent a year and we are able also to dematerialise by 3 percent a year, then we would get economic growth with no (approximately) net increase in environmental impact. If it were possible to sustain this for 50 years, the size of our economy would grow by 340 percent while its impact on the environment would stay the same as day one. That is "sustainable" development.

Dematerialisation is a not a new concept. A number of organizations and individuals have presented studies indicating the potential for major improvements in resource productivity; for example, the "Factor 10 Club" has called for a ten-fold improvement in resource productivity in industrialised countries over the next 30-50 years, whereas von Weizsäcker et al. (1997) have suggested a short-term target of a four-fold improvement.

Three things need to be understood about dematerialisation. First, it should not be a fixed target, like "10-fold". It needs to be expressed as a rate, such as "4 percent a year" because balancing the environmental impacts of economic growth is a dynamic rather than a static process.

66

Second, how much or how fast we need to dematerialise does not have to be arbitrary. It can be determined scientifically. The rate needed to maintain sustainability is governed by the relationship:

dematerialisation rate = economic growth rate

Third, dematerialisation is a fundamental requirement of sustainable development. The environmental impacts associated with economic growth need to be balanced by at least an equal rate of dematerialisation. Simply put, if we can achieve this we will be sustainable. If not, we will not.

3.0   Environmental Considerations in the Information Age

How might the information age impact upon our pursuit of sustainability? Most commentaries so far have been favorable, expecting it to reduce the material intensity of our economic activities significantly, thereby making positive contributions to the environment. Caution is called for, however. The information age may worsen environmental conditions, at least in the short run, before improvements occur. The following are some possible environmental challenges and opportunities that may emerge.

Economic Growth and Sustainability

A 100 million-fold increase in information power will raise productivity, encouraging faster economic growth and potentially exert greater pressure on the environment. Quoting from Schwartz and Leyden (1997) in the July issue of Wired magazine:

> *"Historians will look back on our era as an extraordinary moment. They will chronicle the 40 years from 1980 to 2020 as the key years of a remarkable transformation. In the developed countries of the West, new technologies will lead to big productivity increases that will cause high economic growth ... And then the relentless process of globalization, the opening up of national economies and the integration of markets, will drive the growth through much of the rest of the world."* (pg 115)

This issue of Wired magazine went on to liken our present age to the years following the World War II, a time of booming economic development. Between 1950 and 1973, the world economy grew at an average rate of 4.9 percent. Today we are looking at many of the similar forces at work, if not more powerful ones. Technological advances, globalisation, deregulation and entrepreneurship are all marching forward in unprecedented ways. World GDP growth in the last three years has already picked up, increasing from 2.3 to 2.6 to 3.1 per cent respectively.

If productivity gains in the information age indeed promote GDP growth toward the 5 percent attained in the post-World War II period, the urgency of balancing economic growth and management of the environment would be the foremost sustainability issue. As an example, with a 2 percent GDP growth, the world economy expands by about 2.7 times in 50 years, at 4 percent growth, the figure is 7.1 times.

Dematerialisation

Increased economic growth would mean much higher dematerialisation requirements. There are individual cases cited where substantial dematerialisation has occurred or would be relatively easy to accomplish. But the effect we are looking for would have to be industry-wide, sector-wide, countrywide and, ultimately, worldwide. What progress has been made in dematerialisation? The answer is "to date, not very much".

One indicator is changes in energy intensity, which is one of the few dematerialisation "measures" recorded. According to statistics from the US Department of Energy over the last 25 years energy intensity has been improving at a rate of about 1.2 percent a year in the industrialized countries (Figure 3). A continuation at this rate would be insufficient to make a demonstrable difference in moving towards dematerialisation.

To meet the dematerialisation challenge of the information age, greater reliance is likely to be placed on technology. However, dematerialisation at, for example, 4 percent a year cannot be assumed as consistently achievable, even for information age technologies.

Technology

In the information age answers to environmental problems will come increasingly from technologies in general, rather than those targeted specifically at the environment, such as energy conservation, renewable energy, pollution control and cleaner production. Environment-specific technologies usually focus on the "reduction" side, while greater improvements may well come from the "substitution" and "creation" side where wholesale changes are associated not only with new technologies but also new sourcing, production and distribution systems made possible and necessary by the information age.

There are already signs that efficiency and dematerialisation are increasingly the result of competitive rather than explicit environmental considerations. One implication of this is that it would be more useful to steer the "major" technologies toward sustainability rather than developing specialty technologies just for environmental purposes. This suggests that technologies should be defined in sustainability terms, which is broader than just the environment.

A set of indices might be developed for this purpose. These indices could be applied at the R&D stage, and in government funded R&D projects. Life Cycle Analysis (LCA) is a good starting point, but the fundamental flaw about LCA is that it emphasises pollution reduction. Environmental impacts and wastes from the "cradle to the grave" are negative elements to be minimized. In the information age, the positive substitution possibilities may be more useful in promoting dematerialisation and sustainability.

Environmental Activism of Different Stakeholders

Technologies are the product of market forces. In the pursuit of sustainability, greater reliance will need to be placed on environmental policy instruments such as economic incentives, resource pricing, "green" taxes and voluntary agreements. However, the most powerful market and competition-based measures may not be monetary in nature. They are built upon the environment's increasing influence on the relationship between businesses and their customers. Since the Rio "Earth Summit", there is little doubt that the business sector has taken the largest stride toward sustainability. Environmental Management Systems (EMS), Responsible Care, company environmental reports are just some of the initiatives promoted and implemented by business and industry.

Voluntary environmental measures undertaken by companies are likely to be both more numerous and their performance to be more closely monitored. Increasingly, quantitative goals will need to be set in order to quantify progress. A company's environmental performance is increasingly likely to be judged on how its growth is balanced by its progress in dematerialisation.

A major driving force for implementing environmental measures, be they voluntary or otherwise, will be environmental activism on the part of internal (workers, shareholders) and external (banks and insurers, NGOs, community associations, consumers) stakeholders. Notwithstanding this, the most influential environmental groups in the information age will be those that understand technology and have the capacity to analyse critically the relationship between technology and sustainability in order to influence public policy.

Issues Associated with the Process of Globalisation

With information power accelerating at a rate of 10 times every 2 years, technological innovations will be further led by the industrialised countries. Not only do these countries have to show leadership by adopting technologies that promote dematerialisation but also they need to ensure that these technologies are transferred to developing countries in a timely and effective manner so that economic growth in these latter countries occurs with the least environmental harm.

North-South technology transfer is now primarily through private commercial arrangements rather than through public channels. This pattern is likely to be reinforced in the information age. At the Rio "Earth Summit" it was estimated that US$125 billion in additional development assistance would be needed to promote sustainable development in developing countries. In the intervening period, however, private capital flows have exceeded official development assistance. Ten years ago, private capital was only about 30 percent of all North-South capital flows. Today it is 80 percent, and the total amount is approximately US$ 230 billion a year. Important catalysts in this shift have been deeper and wider liberalisation of trade and investment regimes, as well as increased opportunities for foreign direct investment in privatised assets.

As recipients, developing countries need to promote an enabling policy framework. This includes regulatory reform to remove unnecessary barriers to trade and investment, the adoption of national treatment provisions for investors, the strengthening of corporate governance and clear legislation covering, *inter alia*, taxation, capital movements, contracts and property rights.

North-South Equity

How would sustainability impact upon growth in a North-South context? A "back-of-the envelope" analysis based on the "economic growth equal to dematerialisation" requirement for sustainability was made using the simplified North-South data shown in Table 1. A US$10,000 per capita income differentiation was used rather than an OECD-non-OECD division.

Figure 4 shows the sustainable North-South growth rate under a 4 percent a year dematerialisation scenario. The curve itself represents cases where combined North-South growth rates equal the dematerialisation rate. All points to the right of the curve indicate unsustainable growth while those to the left are sustainable. Figure 5 shows a family of curves for different dematerialisation scenarios.

5.0 The Underlying Challenge

The most striking feature of these graphs is how everything seems to happen within a narrow band of Northern growth rates. Small changes on the side of developed countries would have important effects for developing countries. It also indicates how a reduction in the consumption patterns of the developed countries could have a positive influence on progress towards sustainability.

Indeed, we have so far addressed only the left-hand side of the "dematerialisation rate equal to economic growth rate" equation. If we look back into history, we find that each new generation of technologies has always been more efficient, more environmentally-friendly and more dematerialising. Information age technologies are not unique in this respect. The problem is that new technologies have tended to increase the economic growth side of the equation a lot more than the dematerialisation side. To achieve sustainability, this pattern needs to be reversed. This is the real challenge.

BIBLIOGRAPHY

AYRES, R. U., et al., 1995: Achieving Eco-efficiency in Business. Report to the World Business Council for Sustainable Development, March 1995

BROWN, A., 1997: "Into Productivity Hyperdrive" in Tomorrow Magazine, Vol. VII No. 4 (July-August 1997)

GILDER, G., forthcoming: *Telecoms*.

KELLY, K., 1997: "New Rules for the New Economy" in Wired (September, 1997): pg 140

SCHMIDT-BLEEK, F., 1995: "Increasing Resource Productivity on the Way to Sustainability" in UNEP Industry and Environment (October-December 1995)

SCHWARTZ, P. and LEYDEN, P., 1997: "The Long Boom: A History of the Future 1980-2020" in Wired (July, 1997): pg 115

U.S. DEPARTMENT OF ENERGY (Energy Information Administration), 1997: *International Energy Outlook 1997*. U.S. Department of Energy. Washington D.C.

VON WEIZSACKER, E. et al, 1997: *Factor Four*. Earthscan Publications. London.

Figure 1: Growth in Semiconductor Performance

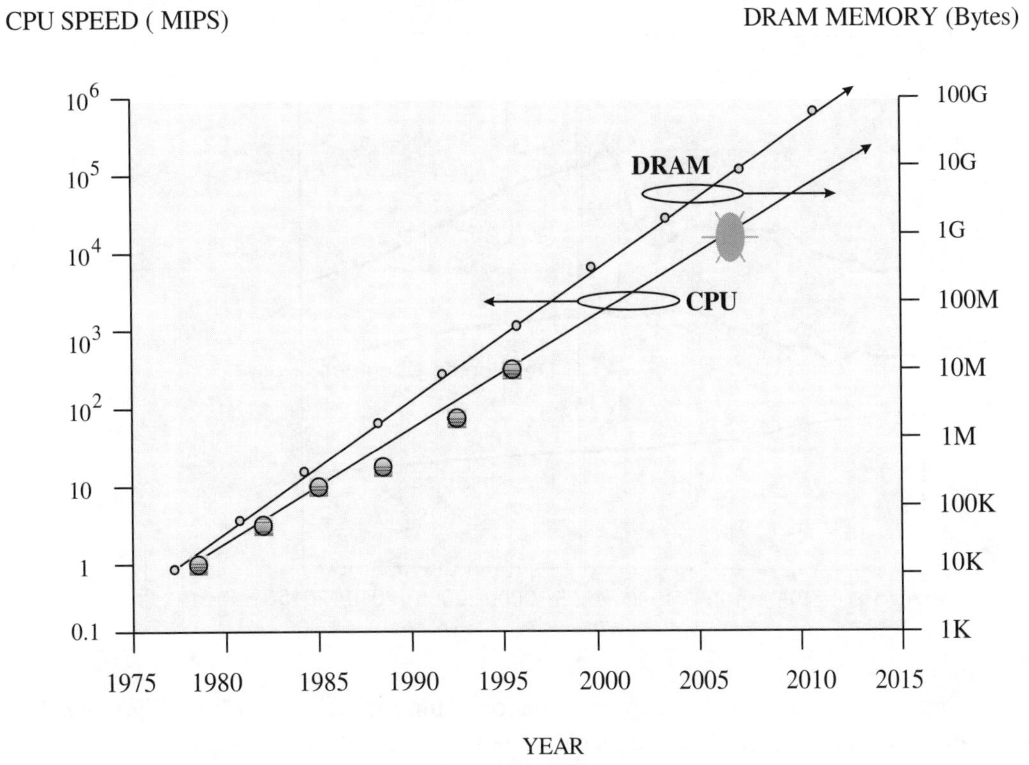

CPU SPEED (MIPS)   DRAM MEMORY (Bytes)

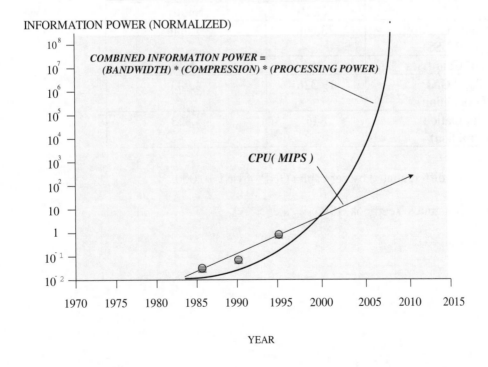

Figure 2: Growth in Combined Information Power

INFORMATION POWER (NORMALIZED)

COMBINED INFORMATION POWER =
(BANDWIDTH) * (COMPRESSION) * (PROCESSING POWER)

CPU(MIPS)

YEAR

Figure 3: Energy Intensity by Region, 1970-2015

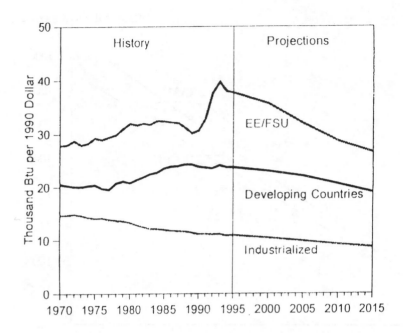

Source: US Department of Energy (Energy Information Administration), 1997: *International Energy Outlook 1997*. (April 1997). US Department of Energy. Washington D.C.

Table 1: North - South Characteristics

	North	South
Average Per Capita GNP(US$)	**23,000**	**1,000**
No. of Countries	48	169
Total GNP (US$ billion)	19,326	4,983
Population (million)	846	4,823

North and South differentiated by per capita GNP of US$ 10,000.

Data Source: Britannica Yearbook, 1996

**Figure 4: Relationship between North-South Growth Rates for a 4% Annual
Dematerialisation Rate, Equivalent to a 7.11 times Dematerialisation in 50 years**

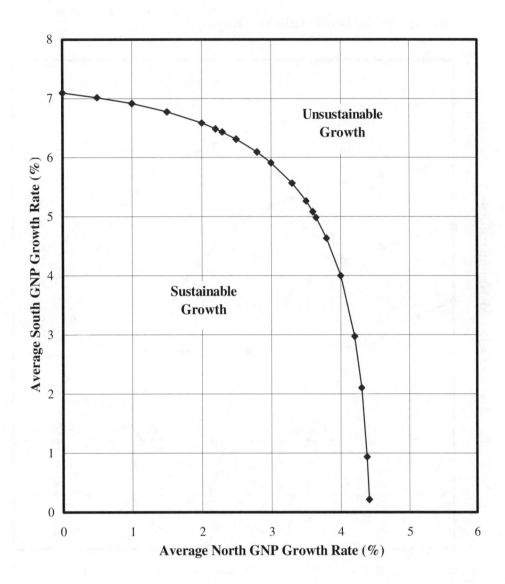

Figure 5: Maximum Sustainable Growth at Various Dematerialisation Rates

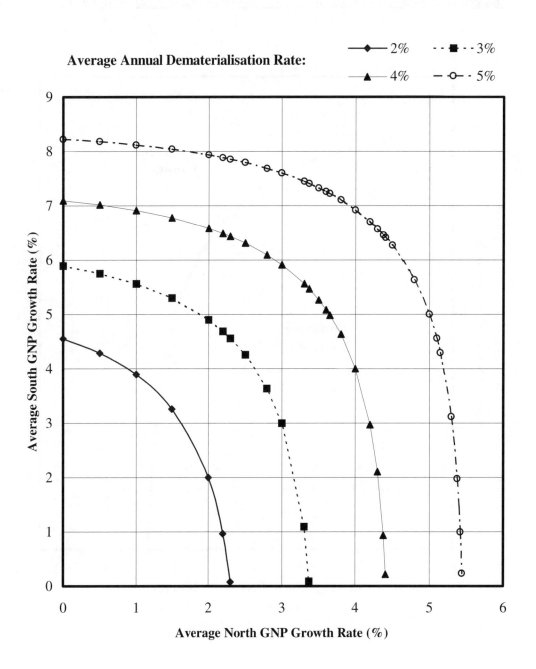

GREEN PURCHASING: A CHANNEL FOR IMPROVING THE ENVIRONMENTAL PERFORMANCE OF SMEs

Burton Hamner and Teresita del Rosario
Asian Institute of Management, the Philippines

1.0 Introduction

Small and Medium-Sized Enterprises (SMEs) are an important industrial sector in most economies, but they create a significant amount of environmental damage, particularly in developing countries. Globalisation is increasing the amount of purchasing by developed country companies from SMEs in developing and rapidly industrializing countries. Many western companies and governments now use environmental criteria in their purchasing. Some types of environmental purchasing, particularly the use of environmental surveys and audits of suppliers, can strongly motivate the suppliers to improve their environmental performance. In the Dynamic Non-Member Economies (DNMEs) of Asia and Latin America, this kind of pressure from buyers may be a particularly effective driver for improved environmental performance of SMEs. This paper considers SMEs in Asia as an analogue for SMEs in the DNMEs generally since their environmental problems seem to cluster around several common areas. Factors affecting their general economic performance are described. Green purchasing strategies and their affect on Asian SMEs are also described, and suggestions are made about the impact of various green purchasing strategies on the environmental performance by Asian SMEs. It is concluded that green purchasing criteria involving supplier surveys and auditing are critical for motivating better environmental performance of SMEs, and should be strongly promoted to OECD companies or governments that purchase goods and services from SMEs in Asia and in general. The final section of the paper presents recommendations for OECD and other international organizations.

2.0 Profile of SMEs in the Asian Region

Definition

There is no consensus on the definition of SMEs throughout the Asia-Pacific region due to the differences in general economic development among countries and their prevailing social conditions. Various indices are used by member economies, among them:

- number of employees[1];
- invested capital;
- total amount of assets;
- sales volume; and
- production capability.

Other classifications exist, contributing to confusion in definition. For example, in China, a distinction is made between SMEs and Township and Village Enterprises (TVEs). In Chinese Taipei, definitions vary with respect to those that expect to receive government assistance. Singapore classifies according to local and overseas SMEs.

Role and Importance of SMEs

There is a widespread recognition that SMEs play a significant role in the economic development of their respective economies. The most important contribution lies in the area of employment. In China, Chinese Taipei, Japan and Thailand, SMEs employ over 70% of the workforce. Data on other Asian economies are shown in Table 1. However, as the Table illustrates some of the data are dated and there are deficiencies in data coverage.

SMEs constitute a large share of the industry sector in their countries' economies. For example:

- Thailand (1991):   98.63%
- Indonesia (1993):   97%
- Philippines (1988):   98.7%.

SMEs also play a strong role in upgrading indigenous enterprises, and contribute significantly to the share of exports. In the case of Chinese Taipei, for example, 55% of exports is contributed by SMEs.

Difficulties Encountered by Asian SMEs

SMEs in different Asian economies experience different problems impacting on their operations. A listing of the most common is shown below:[2]

Export-related

- tariff and non-tariff measures in overseas markets (Hong Kong, China; Korea)
- limited labor pool (Singapore; Malaysia)
- lack of market access (Hong Kong, China; Philippines)
- small volume of goods (Malaysia)

---

[1]   This is the most commonly used index to define SMEs. Number of employees range from 10 to 500.

[2]   APEC, 1994: *The APEC Survey on Small and Medium Enterprises*. APEC. Singapore.

- lack of market information (Indonesia; Philippines)

Overseas Investment

- passive investment attitude (Korea)
- lack of orientation and experience (Indonesia)
- limited capital and other resources (Hong Kong, China; Philippines)
- restrictive investment policy in other countries (Hong Kong, China)
- difficulty in managing workers abroad (Hong Kong, China; Korea)
- inadequate infrastructure in recipient countries (Hong Kong, China)
- keen competition in overseas markets (Hong Kong, China; Philippines)

Industrial Upgrading

- R & D risks (Hong Kong, China)
- low technology capabilities (Indonesia)
- financial constraints (Philippines; Malaysia)
- unavailability of skills (Philippines)

Table 1: The Role of SMEs in Selected Asian Economies

ECONOMY	% SMEs	% EMPLOYED BY SMEs	% SALES VOLUME BY SMEs
Australia	95% (1991-1992) (Small business only)	50.6% (1991-1992) (Small business only)	
China		84.27%	69.49%
Hong Kong, China	97.95% (1993)	63% (1993)	
Indonesia	97% (1993)		
Japan	99.1% (1991)	79.2% (1991)	
Korea	99.8% (1992)	78.5% (1991)	45.9% (mining & manufacturing only, 1992)
Philippines	98.7% (1988)	50% (1988)	26.3% (1988)
Singapore	91.42% (1991)	44% (1991)	
Chinese Taipei	96.77% (1992)	68.63% (1992)	33.66% (1992)
Thailand	98.63% (1991)	73.80% (1991)	

Source: APEC, 1994: *The APEC Survey on Small and Medium Enterprises*. APEC. Singapore.

Some Successful Practices for Promoting SMEs

Governments in Asia have applied a range of strategies to promote SMEs. No single practice seems to be the best or fully adequate; rather, the use of multiple strategies is needed to help SMEs overcome the various obstacles they face.[3] Examples of strategies that have been adopted include:

- China: A supporting industrial policy framework; rationalized distribution among large, medium and small enterprises.

- Japan: Special financial assistance to SMEs.

- Philippines: Guarantee fund for SMEs; second level guarantee (reinsurance); lending institutions set aside a portion of total portfolio for SME lending.

- Chinese Taipei: A comprehensive assistance system based on:

  -- a credit guarantee fund;
  -- management support to improve operational efficiency and to develop human resources;
  -- production technology assistance to guide and assist SMEs in adopting new technologies and to receive training;
  -- support for research and development to encourage the development of new products and technologies;
  -- information management to assist SMEs in effectively accessing and using information on current and potential markets;
  -- promotion of pollution prevention and industrial safety.

Summary

There are many definitions and classifications of SMEs throughout Asia but the most commonly used is number of employees: 10-500 is the average number. There is widespread consensus on the role and significance of SMEs in the economic development of particular countries in terms of generating opportunities for growth and upgrading indigenous enterprises.

While this role has been accepted, there are a number of significant problems that prevent SMEs from realizing their full potential. Among them are lack of finance, human resource problems, low technology, and lack of market information and export market access. In general, very few SMEs have the capacity to engage in export, mostly because of their inability to compete with larger enterprises and also because of the risks involved. (Chinese Taipei is an exception. Its export base in SMEs is 55%.) In order to address the problems, the general industrial policy framework is considered an important component, together with financial assistance from governments and industry itself.

---

[3]   Tan, Q., 1995: *The Philippine SME Situationer: Status, Prospects and Outlook.* Canadian International Development Agency. Ottawa.

3.0   Globalisation, SMEs and the Environment

While "analysis so far has concluded that trade liberalization will be generally beneficial for environmental quality,"[4] no firm conclusions can be drawn about the impact on environmental performance of any particular country, industry sector, or level of company size. The impact on SMEs in particular has not been widely addressed. Yet SMEs are of particular concern for environmental management. Because they have less capital, investments in pollution control are less affordable for SMEs. In addition, because they are large in number and low in individual visibility, governments have a difficult time monitoring them. And because they are often located in highly urbanised areas, the impact of their pollution on human health can be serious and immediate.

SMEs in Asia and elsewhere can significantly reduce their pollution and increase their profits through training in, and advice on, cleaner production methods. For example, from 1992 to 1996, the U.S. Agency for International Development sponsored a project in the Philippines called the Industrial Environmental Management Project (IEMP). This project included a cleaner production component and waste minimisation training that involved 140 SMEs in Pollution Management Appraisals.[5] The objective of these appraisals was to help the companies identify low- and no-cost ways to reduce their pollution through process improvements with positive playback. By March 1996, the project had achieved the following results:

Table 2: Results from 140 Philippine SMEs Participating in Pollution Management Appraisals (US$)

Indicator	Target	Achieved
Investments by Firms	Not defined	$21,500,000
Annualised Net Benefits	$800,000	$31,400,000
Pollution Reduction (BOD)	5-10%	33%
Water Use Reduction	Not defined	33,000,000 m^3/yr
Firms Adopting Waste Minimisation	50%	98%

Similar results have been obtained from other cleaner production and pollution prevention programs in Asia[6]. These clearly demonstrate that SMEs can improve their environmental performance if they are motivated to try and are given basic training in cleaner production assessment methods.

Most Asian economies have well-developed environmental regulatory regimes. However the robust enforcement of environmental regulations remains a major challenge for most of them. Among the Asian DNMEs, Singapore has arguably the most consistent and effective record in

---

[4]   Adams, J., 1997: "Globalization, Trade and the Environment" in OECD (1997):
Globalization and the Environment: Preliminary Perspectives. OECD, Paris.

[5]   Philippine Industry's Response to Waste Minimization. Environmental Management Bureau, Philippine Department of Environment and Natural Resources, Manila, 1996.

[6]   See OECD, 1997: *Cleaner Production and Waste Minimisation in OECD and Dynamic Non-Member Economies.* OECD Document Series. OECD. Paris.

enforcement. Chinese Taipei, Malaysia and Hong Kong, China have "medium" effective enforcement. In most other economies of the region enforcement is generally weak. Companies that violate pollution standards can often continue doing so even after the government has ordered them to stop because the legal system and national environmental authorities do not have sufficient power or resources to ensure that decisive action is undertaken. Large companies generally comply relatively well because of their visibility, high individual pollution discharges, and resources for pollution control. Greater difficulty is experienced with SMEs. Even when SMEs have installed pollution control equipment it is often not used because of the high operating expense.

Pressure from government can usually be ignored, and local communities often do not demand controls because they fear the potential loss of jobs (which the companies invariably threaten). Given these realities, what factors might motivate SMEs to improve their environmental performance?

4.0 Green Purchasing and SMEs: A Vital Channel for Promoting Environmental Sustainability

Green purchasing is the practice of applying environmental criteria to the selection of products or services. It takes a number of forms, from relatively simple to more complex (see section 5 below). Green purchasing is now quite common among larger companies and appears to be increasingly used as a corporate practice. For example, a 1995 survey of 1000 buyers of office equipment and supplies showed that 80% of respondents were taking part in environmental initiatives within their organizations. In 1993, just 40% of respondents responded this way.[7] Most readers will themselves know of organizations that are using environmental criteria of some sort in purchasing.

Green purchasing practices are being increasingly documented in the academic literature as well as in numerous case studies and books on environmental management.[8,9,10,11,12] The U.K. organization, Business in the Environment, has published a training kit for promoting environmental

---

[7] Avery, S., 1995: "Buyers Go Green – Slowly" in Purchasing 119(4): pp43-45.

[8] Drumwright, M., 1994: "Socially Responsible Organizational Buying: Environmental Concern as a Noneconomic Buying Criterion" in Journal of Marketing 58(8): pp 1-19.

[9] Sarkis, J., 1995: "Supply Chain Management and Environmentally Conscious Design and Manufacturing" in International Journal of Environmentally Conscious Design and Manufacturing 4(2): pp 43-52.

[10] Lamming, R. and Hampson, J., 1996: "The Environment as a Supply Chain Management Issue" in British Journal of Management, 7: Special Issue (March): pp 45-62.

[11] Lloyd, M., 1994: "How Green Are My Suppliers? – Buying Environmental Risk" in Purchasing and Supply Management (October 1994): pp 36-39.

[12] Tyler, G., 1997: "Blueprint for Green Supplies" in Supply Management 2(7): pp 36-38.

management to suppliers.[13] The U.S. National Association of Purchasing Managers has a committee on environmental purchasing, and the topic is a regular feature of their conferences. A survey of 256 U.S. manufacturing firms, which asked the firms to identify the key players in their pollution prevention strategies, revealed that nearly half identified suppliers as such.[14]

Some of the leading Multi-National Corporations (MNCs) whose international supplier environmental management efforts are described in the literature include Motorola, IBM, S.C. Johnson, TRW, Nokia, Sony, Ford, Ray-O-Vac, Northern Telecom, Apple Computer, Sun Microsystems, and the Body Shop. Many more companies with domestic supplier environmental programs are also described.

What effect is this having? The impact on international suppliers, especially in developing countries, is not yet well documented but there is increasing evidence that the impact on suppliers is significant:

> *"Denim producer Arvind Mills Ltd., based in Ahmedabad, is plowing $16 million into new pollution control devices – in part to satisfy customer Marks and Spencer. And after New Delhi-based pharmaceutical Ranbaxy Laboratories was queried on environmental standards by Hoechst, it decided to upgrade all its manufacturing sites to make them "zero discharge" sites. Says Ranbaxy health and environment adviser Prafull Sheth: "If you are not manufacturing your products taking care of the environment, your products may not be acceptable."*[15]

One of us (Hamner) has worked closely with two international apparel companies, Nike Inc. and Gap, Inc., to help train their Asian suppliers in approaches to pollution prevention and cleaner production. The two companies required their suppliers to participate in these workshops as a condition of continuing existing contractual relationships. Although the suppliers who attended expressed strong concerns about the costs of meeting environmental standards imposed by their buyers, all indicated that they would do so. They were also very interested in cleaner production as an alternative to pollution control in order to meet the standards.

In August 1997 the only company in the Philippines certified to the ISO 14001 Environmental Management Systems standard was Texas Instruments, Inc. in the city of Bagio. The company's environmental manager informed the authors that the major reason they decided to achieve certification is that one of their major Japanese customers told them it would be required eventually of all their suppliers. The customer also conducted an environmental audit of the facility. Another Asian manufacturer, Lucent Technologies (formerly part of AT&T) has made a commitment to ISO 14001 certification partly in order to satisfy major Japanese electronics companies that it supplies.

---

[13] Business in the Environment, 1995: *Environmental Management: A Supplier's Guide.*
Business in the Environment. London.

[14] Florida, R., 1996: "Lean and Green: The Move to Environmentally Conscious Manufacturing" in California Management Review 39(1): 80-105.

[15] "Clean Up or Shut Down: India's Courts Get Tough With Industries That Pollute" in Business Week (Asia Edition), 29 September, 1997.

5.0   Green Purchasing Strategies and Impact on Suppliers

There is a range of green purchasing strategies available to multi-national corporations (MNCs). Different strategies have different effects on the environmental behaviour of suppliers. The strategies can be grouped into three major categories: product standards, behavior standards, and collaboration (see Box 1).

The effect of the various strategies on supplier environmental performance tends to follow a continuum from low (product standards) to high (collaboration). For example, specifying product standards is not likely to change a supplier's behaviour since the supplier only has to change ingredients. At the other end of the continuum, collaborating with suppliers on environmental issues is almost certain to change the supplier's behaviour. This also requires much more effort by the buyers. In general, more effort by buyers is needed to increase the environmental performance of suppliers. Thus buyers must make a cost-benefit analysis regarding how much they want their suppliers to improve.

Box 1: Green Purchasing Strategies

Product Standards

- Purchase products that have environmentally-friendly attributes, e.g. recycled materials, non-toxic ingredients.
- Purchase products that disclose their environmental attributes, e.g. eco-labeling.

Behaviour Standards

- Require suppliers to disclose information about their environmental practices, pollution discharges, etc.
- Audit suppliers to evaluate their environmental performance.
- Require suppliers to implement and maintain an environmental management system (EMS).
- Require suppliers to obtain certification of their EMS.
- Require suppliers to have an EMS that meets recognised standards, such as EMAS, ISO 14001, Responsible Care, etc.

Collaboration

- Work with suppliers to help them reduce environmental impacts through changes in product design and materials use.
- Implement product stewardship programmes throughout all stages of a product's life cycle.

The use of environmental management standards will not it itself necessarily improve suppliers' environmental performance. This depends on the standard being applied. For example, ISO 14001 does not require improvements in environmental performance, whereas the EMAS standard does.[16] Thus buyers who choose the "low cost" strategy of simply requiring suppliers to meet some external standard for behaviour or environmental management need to consider which standard best reflects their environmental goals.

Imposing a certification standard on an SME supplier may have negative effects. Obtaining certification is time-consuming and expensive. SMEs may obtain greater financial and environmental benefits by spending that time and money on process improvements rather than developing an environmental management system with its supporting bureaucracy. In the worst case an SME might be forced out of business because it does not have the time and money needed to meet buyer environmental requirements.

There is some evidence that simply asking a supplier about its environmental performance is enough to galvanise the supplier to act, as noted in the Business Week quote above. However, this is unlikely to be an effective approach given the absence of continuous pressure by, or technical support for improvement from, the buyer.

Lamming and Hampson (1996) studied four large U.K. companies that applied environmental criteria and demands to their suppliers. They noted that:

> *"In general, the response of suppliers to initial customer proposals to make improvements in environmental soundness was reported to be cool … Broadly, suppliers responded to [environmental] problems only in so far as the customer companies required them to do so, indicating that the area is very market- driven."[17]*

This general response should be considered in relation to the range of green purchasing strategies available. The evidence indicates that it takes direct communication from buyers for suppliers to take environmental issues seriously. Yet most organizations that include environmental criteria in purchasing limit themselves to product standards. They may assume that such standards promote environmental improvement up the supply chain but this is not likely to be the case. Active involvement is needed to ensure true improvements.

Active involvement, however, costs time and money. Is there a bottom-line justification for active involvement with suppliers on environmental issues? The majority of companies that collaborate with suppliers on environmental improvement state that their rationale is better business, not a better environment *per se*. The U.K. retailer B&Q provides one example:

---

[16]   Nash, J., 1997: "ISO 14000: Evolution, Scope and Limitations" in Tibor and Feldman (eds) *Implementing ISO 14000.* Irwin Publishing.

[17]   Lamming, R. and Hampson, J., 1996: see Footnote 10.

"We decided to work with the supplier to provide health and safety expertise at a new factory the supplier was building. With this help the supplier was not only able to manufacture products in far safer conditions but by reducing the level of dust, for example, product quality was of a higher standard. Production efficiencies also enabled B&Q to negotiate better prices from the supplier, so all parties were winners - employees, the supplier and B&Q." [18]

Apple Computer was faced with the need to eliminate CFCs from its products. It worked closely with suppliers to develop a new process for circuit board production that eliminated the need for cleaning completely. This not only reduced pollution at suppliers' factories, but also eliminated a production bottleneck and increased productivity.

The business benefits of working closely with suppliers as strategic partners have been well documented. [19] Companies that collaborate with suppliers in solving environmental problems will benefit in general from improved communications, systems integration, planning and research. Specific environmental benefits include reduction of environmental risks and liability, improved supply reliability and lower pollution control costs (which is passed on eventually to buyers). In summary, the effort and cost to buyers of collaborating with suppliers on environmental improvement will generally be offset by the general and specific benefits accruing from better business partnerships.

6.0   Challenges to Collaboration

There are of course obstacles to working closely with suppliers. The leverage of buyers to influence suppliers depends on a number of factors, including volume of purchases, ability to integrate operations throughout the supply chain, switching costs, and others. [20]   The type of relationship between buyers and suppliers varies widely. SME exporters most likely have an arms-length relationship with their overseas buyers and may not expect any visits from their buyers. SME suppliers to MNCs in their own countries are much more likely to be involved in complex relationships with, and subject to, inspection by their customers.

One example of the difficulty of pushing environmental behavior up the supply chain comes from the Asian textile industry. Firms that dye and print fabrics buy the "gray" fabric from weavers who add starch sizings during weaving to make the yarn more pliable. The customers must wash the fabric to remove the starch before they can dye or print on the fabric. The BOD in the resulting wastewater is one of the most significant pollution discharges of the dyeing/printing industry. Weavers often use much more sizing than is really necessary, so the BOD in their customers' wastewater is also higher than necessary. An obvious approach is to get the weavers to

---

[18]   Green, K. and Morton, B., 1996: Green Purchasing and Supply Policies: Do They Improve Companies' Environmental Performance? Paper Presented at 5th International Conference of the Greening of Industry Network, Heidelberg, Germany, November 1996.

[19]   Lewis, J., 1995: *The Connected Corporation: How Leading Companies Win Through Customer-Supplier Alliances.* Free Press.

[20]   Porter, M., 1985: *Competitive Advantage.* Free Press.

minimize sizing applications, which would reduce the customers' water pollution load and also save the weavers money on sizing materials.

The customers buy gray fabric from weaving companies all over the world, however. In many cases in Asia fabric is purchased from a consolidator or broker acting as a middleman. In most cases the company with the wastewater problem is one or two steps removed from the supplier who actually creates the pollution problem, and the buyer does not purchase sufficient quantity from any one supplier to have leverage in requesting environmental improvements. In this case, the power of buyers to demand environmental improvements from their suppliers is low.

In contrast, the Asian semiconductor industry generally involves very close relationships between suppliers and buyers. This is because the very precise production tolerances and rapid changes in technology require that buyers regularly inspect and work with their suppliers on quality and technology. The tight competition among suppliers for big customers means that customers have a lot of leverage. Some buyers even have full-time representatives at their supplier's factories. In the cases where the buyers have well-developed environmental management programs, they are extending these programs to cover their suppliers since the marginal cost of doing so is quite low. Companies such as Lucent Technologies, Nokia, Apple Computer and Hewlett Packard are actively working in this way with their suppliers.

7.0   Globalisation and Greening the Supply Chain

Globalisation increases the opportunities for buyers to source from SMEs in an increasing number of countries. As buyers increase their focus on environmental improvement, the issue of supplier environmental performance will increase in importance. This is particularly true for organizations that regard environmental improvement as a social goal, not just an issue of cost, risk and public image.

Companies

Companies (and any organisation that conducts purchasing activities, including governments) should decide what are their real environmental goals regarding extra-organisational environmental improvement. Even though an organisation may have a policy to promote environmental sustainability, in practice environmental improvement is often focused on internal risk reduction. For example, a recent study of the green purchasing practices of members of the National Association of Purchasing Managers showed that "current green purchasing strategies seem to be reactive in that they try to avoid violations of environmental statutes rather than embedding environmental goals within the business' long-term corporate strategy."[21]

The desire to green the supply chain may be more common among certain types of companies. Drumwright[22] proposes a framework explaining *why* organisations engage in green purchasing. She differentiates organisations into two general categories. The first category (Types I and II) concerns organisations for which green purchasing is a deliberate outcome of articulated

---

[21]   Min , H. and Galle, W., 1997: "Green Purchasing Strategies: Trends and Implications" in International Journal of Purchasing and Materials Management 33: pg 3.

[22]   Drumwright, M., 1994: see Footnote 8.

strategies of socially responsible behaviour. In Type I organisations, green purchasing is an extension of the *founder's ideals*. In Type II organisations, green purchasing is *symbolic* of the corporate mission. The second category (Types III and IV) is organisations in which green purchasing is motivated by basic business reasons. Type III organisations see green purchasing as *opportune*, while Type IV organisations engage in it because of external *restraints*. Drumwright also proposes strategies for vendors who seek business from the four types of organisations.

In her study of the buying processes in 36 firms, Drumwright mentions no obvious correlation between the nature of the business (industry sector, size, etc.) and the type of purchasing motivation she assigned to it. It seems likely that the best predictors of what types of companies would be likely to engage in green purchasing are industry sector, size, and public responsibility. The chemical industry, with its high process and product risks and large-size firms, is likely to be motivated to implement green purchasing because of business reasons and to work closely with suppliers due to its high buyer leverage. Government organisations that respond to public interests fall under Type II, where green purchasing is symbolic of the government's mission to promote sustainability. For SMEs in developing and emerging economies there are no obvious factors that would differentiate green purchasing behavior by type of business.

It is likely that only Type I and II companies will actively pursue improvements in supplier environmental behaviour beyond imposing product standards, since the extra work involved would be values-driven rather than based on economics or risk. Such companies will need to stress to suppliers that good environmental performance is expected and that the level of performance will be considered in selecting suppliers. However, product standards can be effective in achieving some improvements in supplier behaviour, especially if they are applied broadly enough. For example, governments and large corporations that have specified the purchase of recycled paper have stimulated their suppliers to make major investments in recycling facilities. In this case the product standard (recycled paper content) was uniform enough and the demand was large enough to affect suppliers significantly.

If companies really want to promote environmental sustainability through purchasing, they will need to recognize that simple strategies such as focusing on product ingredients is not likely to have a significant external effect. They will need to reinforce to suppliers that good environmental performance is integral to their business operation and that the level of performance is a factor in maintaining long-term contractual relationships with suppliers.

Globalisation means that suppliers will increasingly be located in countries other than those of their product buyers. Buyers will need to educate themselves about the environmental conditions, regulations and other factors in supplier countries. If the supplier is in a country with well-enforced environmental regulations, the buyer may have some confidence that the supplier is subject to regular monitoring. But if the country's environmental regulations are lax or poorly enforced, the buyer should begin with the assumption that the supplier may be a serious polluter and potentially a source of environmental liability. This assumption is particularly applicable when the suppliers are SMEs. In these situations buyers should ask suppliers to provide documentation regarding pollution discharges, environmental health and safety controls, etc. Where possible, suppliers should be visited to inspect their operations.

Governments

A recent OECD study has documented the many ways OECD Member country governments are now using environmental criteria in purchasing.[23] Governments are the largest buyers of products and services. Thus government purchasing policies focused on environmental performance can have a more direct effect than any other type of environmental pressure. Governments may be constrained in the selection of suppliers by rules regarding low bid selection; nonetheless, suppliers can be questioned regarding their environmental performance.

It is not clear whether government policies can influence the purchasing behaviour of other organisations, or even if this is desirable. However, governments can act as an advocate for improved buyer-supplier relationships and can document examples of "best practice" for dissemination. Governments also need to decide how strongly they will apply criteria for supplier environmental behaviour, as well as product standards.

Trade and Business Associations

Trade and business associations have a particularly significant role to play in "greening" the supply chain. Since these groups are very familiar with the environmental issues in their specific industry they are in an excellent position to help their members identify the key issues and to share strategies about how to work with suppliers. For example, the American Electronics Association has a number of work groups and conferences focused on environmental management, and supplier management is a regular topic.

A major obstacle in greening the supply chain is the bargaining power of individual buyers. If a buyer is not very important to a supplier, requests for environmental improvement will not likely receive a positive response. Through trade and business associations, however, groups of buyers can band together to put pressure on suppliers. This strategy is being used by American apparel companies that have developed a set of wastewater discharge standards that they are applying to their suppliers worldwide. Companies such as Levi-Strauss and Gap may individually only constitute a small proportion of a textile manufacturer's sales. But since the two companies agree on the same pollution standards they have the leverage to demand that a supplier meet the standards, or lose the business of both companies.

8.0   Recommendations

International organisations that promote sustainability, such as OECD, have a number of options to promote greening of the supply chain. However, it is critical that promotion of this concept emphasizes the business reasons for green purchasing and supply chain management. Since improvements in supplier environmental performance are generally only achieved after buyers make a substantial effort to work with them, the buyers must be convinced that there is an economic as well as environmental incentive.

---

[23]   OECD, 1997: Greener Public Purchasing. Issues Paper Prepared for the Green Goods IV International Conference on Greener Public Purchasing, 24-26 February, 1997. Biel-Bienne, Switzerland.

Develop Expertise in Strategic Supply Chain Management

Purchasing is evolving from a line to a strategic function in leading companies. There is ample documentation regarding the business benefits to companies that have implemented collaborative supply chain management systems. Greening the supply chain needs to be considered and presented within the framework of buyer-supplier alliances for improved competitiveness. Economic benefits must be emphasised as much or even more than environmental benefits. OECD should develop expertise in supply chain management as a base from which green purchasing practices and policies can be developed.

Document "Win-Win" Examples of Green Purchasing

Many companies are using some form of green purchasing strategy. This paper has described some examples in which green purchasing has resulted in improvements for both buyers and suppliers. More examples are available and should be compiled into a case collection to be used in promoting collaborative green purchasing.

Promote Green Buying and Supplier Evaluation as Government Purchasing Policy

A number of governments now use environmental criteria in their purchasing. The primary focus of such practices is to increase the use of recycled materials and reduce the use of environmentally harmful materials. However, as discussed earlier, these practices are not likely to push suppliers towards improved environmental performance. The U.K. government provides environmental guidelines for suppliers but does not require them to be followed, although the suppliers' environmental performance may be considered in supplier selection. The common requirement that contracts go to the lowest bidder may be a further obstacle to effective use of environmental criteria in supplier selection.

The use of environmental management standards such as ISO 14001, EMAS, BS 7750, etc. as a criterion for government purchasing is a matter of much debate. No government to date requires suppliers to demonstrate compliance with these standards as a condition of obtaining contracts. Further, whether environmental performance of suppliers is improved through adherence to a standard depends on which standard is followed and the degree to which it emphasises continuous improvements in environmental performance. It is not clear that certification to an environmental management standard will be mandatory in government purchasing contracts because of the expense that certification to a standard might impose on suppliers.

Governments could promote improved supplier environmental performance by requiring suppliers to respond to a detailed questionnaire about their environmental practices and performance. This raises the environment issue to the executive level among suppliers and indicates that it is something that must be addressed strategically in order to remain competitive. The results of such a survey would also provide valuable data in examining progress in implementing policies promoting "green" government purchasing of products and services.

Promote Cleaner Production as a Specific Requirement of Environmental Management Standards

Cleaner production is not specifically required in the most international of the environmental management standards, ISO 14001. In fact, ISO 14001 does not even require that organisations make pollution prevention a priority; it simply requires a policy commitment to "prevention of pollution", and defines "prevention of pollution" to include treatment and control as an alternative to true prevention.

Nonetheless, environmental management standards such as ISO 14001 are likely to become increasingly used by buyers to obtain assurance about supplier environmental performance. Governments therefore should make a specific effort to educate the public and companies about the limitations of environmental management standards as guarantees of improved environmental performance. Specifically, cleaner production and true pollution prevention should be promoted as elements of environmental management standards, although modification of the standards themselves is not feasible

Study and Disseminate "Best Practices" to Help Suppliers Improve Their Environmental Performance

There are numerous examples of suppliers and buyers working together for environmental improvement. However, there have been no systematic studies regarding the impact of various green purchasing strategies on suppliers. Such studies could identify which strategies have the greatest effect at achieving improved environmental performance while increasing economic benefits to both buyers and suppliers. These "best practices" could then be widely promoted and disseminated within industry.

Develop an Environmental Training Program for Corporate Purchasing Departments

There is already at least one environmental training package for suppliers, published by the U.K. organization Business in the Environment. However, this package does not provide training for purchasing managers themselves. It is vital to recall that the person who will implement green purchasing is not the environmental manager, but the purchasing manager. These individuals often need some environmental education before they can begin discussing the issues with suppliers. Once environmental issues are understood, they need to be placed within a strategic purchasing context. Purchasing managers will seldom pursue green strategies if they are not perceived as economically beneficial to the organization. A training program for purchasing managers can be conducted using product life cycle analysis as a framework and supply chain management strategies as the functional elements. Environmental issues can be overlaid on this structure so that they are recognized and managed as business issues.

Target Trade and Business Associations

The most effective channel to promote green purchasing strategies is through trade and business associations. Purchasing managers are most receptive to best practices information that comes from within their own industry. In addition, buyers can form groups to increase their leverage with suppliers on environmental issues.

Industry associations are now becoming strongly focused on global trade issues. Concerns of their members about doing business with suppliers who may be creating severe environmental problems can be placed within a context of a business's strategic response to the challenges and opportunities of globalisation.

9.0   Conclusion

The most uniformly successful way to promote improved environmental performance in SMEs is through the supply chain. No supplier will ignore a justified request from an important buyer who wants to know about the supplier's environmental performance, and such requests demonstrate to suppliers that there is a market incentive to achieve improved environmental performance. There is a small but growing number of companies that have demonstrated that buyer-supplier collaboration on environmental issues results in better economic as well as environmental performance for both parties. Lessons from these experiences should be examined and disseminated widely to business to promote improved environmental management practices. As this paper has shown, multinational enterprises, large companies and governments have a number of opportunities to promote "greening" of the supply chain, including in SMEs, as part of the globalisation process.

GLOBALISATION, THE STATE AND THE ENVIRONMENT

Tom Burke
Rio Tinto plc, United Kingdom

1.0 Introduction

Five key components of the globalisation process can be identified:

- the creation of a global information space, principally through rapid advances in communications technologies;
- the growth in global capital markets;
- the creation of a global market for goods and services;
- an increased role for international 'rules of the game, in particular those on trade and the environment'; and
- the emergence of global values in some areas.

The process of globalisation is neither complete nor homogeneous. There are still many countries that are not strong participants in the global economy, particularly from Africa. The fuller integration of these countries into the global economy represents a major challenge both domestically, where the establishment or strengthening of economic, institutional, legal, social and human capacities is vital, and for the broader international community.

Globalisation is likely to result in different economic, social and environmental outcomes for different groups within and among countries. In this context, the globalisation of opportunity will need to be accompanied by globalisation of responsibility just as nationalisation of opportunity in the latter half of the 19th Century was accompanied by nationalisation of responsibility. It is often overlooked that the emergence of single national markets is a relatively recent phenomenon, driven, as is the globalisation of markets, by significant improvements in communications. It was only after markets became national that national standards on a diverse range of matters from accounting to occupational health began to emerge. The same process of responsibility chasing opportunity will occur as globalisation proceeds.

This paper examines some of the key issues surrounding the evolving role of the state in a globalising economy, in particular the implications for environmental policy. It begins by first describing the environmental policy challenges facing states, and, second, discussing what the state should and should not do in responding to these challenges.

2.0 The Environmental Policy Challenge

At the Rio "Earth Summit" in 1992 there was agreement by heads of state to make the transition to sustainable development. Agenda 21 was endorsed as the 'blueprint' to guide this transition, further supplemented by the Programme for the Further Implementation of Agenda 21 adopted at the June 1997 UN General Assembly Special Session (UNGASS) "Earth Summit+5". Since then a considerable effort has been made at many levels within both public and private institutions to begin shifting both policies and practice on to more sustainable trajectories. [1]

The concept of sustainable development as contained in Agenda 21 contains both an operational and a moral component. The operational component relates to the requirement to ensure that economic development does not undermine the ecological foundations of the economy. The moral component relates to both the need for inter-generational equity and the perception that the political conditions for protecting the ecological foundations of the economy from irreversible degradation cannot be achieved without a greater degree of equity within the present population.

Thus, the transition to sustainable development is a necessary condition for the protection of the ecological foundations of the global economy. Just how dependent we remain for our economic well- being on the productivity of the global ecosystem is often overlooked.

Although fossil fuels and non-fossil minerals play a large part in sustaining economic development, the world's economy remains hugely dependent on other types of natural resources. These resources provide all of our food, much of our fibre, a wide range of chemical and pharmaceutical products, many materials for construction and furniture and a vast range of other goods and services on which the economy depends. A recent estimate set the possible value of these goods and services at between $16 - $54 trillion a year.[2] Clearly, such analysis is in its early stage of development but it provides a useful indicator of the much overlooked scale of their contribution to our economic well being.

The productivity of the non-fossil fuel part of the global economy is dependent on just six bio-geophysical systems which together represent the ecological foundations of the economy:

- croplands;
- rangelands;
- forests;
- freshwater;

---

[1] There have been many attempts to create an operational definition of sustainable development most of which fail because they attempt to define a state rather than a dynamic process. It is probably more useful to think in terms of shifting the trajectory of policy from unsustainable to sustainable modes and therefore to seek to identify demarcation criteria by which to discriminate between unsustainable and sustainable trajectories e.g. a transport policy which seeks to break the linkage between rising real incomes and increased vehicle use is clearly more sustainable than one which does not.

[2] Costanza, R., d'Arge, R., de Groot, R., Farber, S., Grasso, M., Hannon, B., Limburg, K., Naeem, S., O'Neill, R.V.O., Paruelo, J., Raskin, R.G., Sutton, P., van den Belt, M., 1997: "The value of the world's ecosystem services and natural capital" in Nature 387 (6630) (15 May 1997): 253 - 260.

- oceans; and
- the atmosphere.

Any decline in the productivity of these six systems results in a decline in the overall productivity of the global economy although this may be masked for some time by substitution of fossil fuels and non-fossil fuel mineral inputs. Eventually, at different times in different places, limits to substitution are reached and the system locally suffers irreversible degradation in its productivity as can already be seen in many parts of the world.

The challenge of making the transition to sustainable development is to double the population of the planet in fifty years whilst raising real incomes and avoiding further degradation in the productivity of these six environmental systems.

An Evolving Agenda: New Issues, New Politics

Addressing the above challenge will require new approaches in policy analysis and policy-making, involving multiple stakeholders inside and outside government. In this context, it is important to understand the different political dynamics of the "old agenda/easy politics" of the 25 years since the 1972 Stockholm Conference on the Human Environment and the "new agenda/hard politics" that is emerging and which is likely to characterise environmental policy-making in the new millennium (see Table 1).

Table 1: The Evolving Context of Environmental Policy-Making

	1st 25 years	Next 25 years
	Easy Politics/Old Agenda	Hard Politics/New Agenda
Issues	Air and water quality Noise and nuisances Contaminated land Wastes and recycling Toxic chemicals Radioactivity Endangered species	Climate change Food security (Topsoil) Fisheries Forests Biodiversity Access to water Biotechnology, genetically modified organisms
Politics	Need clear More winners than losers Many "win-win" options	Need unclear More losers than winners Fewer "win-win" options, more difficult trade-offs required
Policy Tools	Available	Not available
Public Driver	Threats to public health	Threats to strategic natural resources and "commons" resources
Resolution Mode	Confrontation	Collaboration
Status	Significant progress Tactical gains	Little progress Strategic losses
Impact on Business	Cost of market entry	Market structure
Implications for Business	Mainly technical issue Managing objectivities	Mainly business issue Managing subjectivities
Institutions	Adequate	Inadequate
Geo-politics	Developing country priority	Developed country priority
Economic Significance	Marginal	Central
Media	High Profile	Lower profile

As Table 1 shows, the "old agenda/easy politics" was largely one of pollution control driven by public health concerns. The need for political action was clear, sustained by strong public pressure; there were more winners than losers; and the policy tools, principally regulations and standards, were available and proven.

Issues emerging under the "new agenda/hard politics" are much more complex and their resolution requires difficult economic, social and political trade-offs. The role of international co-operation is also more important as many of the issues relate to the protection and management of shared resources. Several factors reflect the increased complexity of the "new agenda": the impetus for political action is unclear because cause-effect and cost-benefit relationships are much more difficult to isolate and quantify; the time-scale of some of the environmental changes is long and the science is uncertain; the domestic economic and social implications of response strategies have increased in political importance because of competitiveness concerns; public interest and public pressure fluctuates; and the necessary policy instruments and performance evaluation tools are not well developed.

3.0   The Changing Role of the State

The role of the state is evolving in response to, *inter alia*, the process of globalisation and domestic reforms in public sector management and redefined relationships between central and lower levels of government. Emphasis is shifting from the state being a principal provider of public goods and services to one of partner, catalyst and facilitator. At the same time, there is increasing pressure on the state to ensure that (i) its role is matched to its capability, requiring a clearer definition of what it should and should not do, as well as how to do it; and (ii) the performance of public institutions is raised so that efficiency, effectiveness, transparency and accountability are improved[3]. This is forcing governments at all levels (local, regional, national) to think more critically and creatively about their core tasks, to define cost-effective implementation strategies and to establish more objective indicators of performance. Table 2 shows a range of activities and the extent of state intervention, classified as "minimal", "intermediate" and "activist" functions.

Table 2: Functions of the State and Activities

	Addressing Market Failure			Improving Equity
Minimal Functions	Providing pure public goods: • Defence • Law and order • Property rights • Macro-economic management • Public health			Protecting the poor: • Antipoverty programmes • Disaster relief
Intermediate Functions	Addressing externalities: • Basic education • Environment protection	Regulating monopoly: • Utility regulation • Antitrust policy	Overcoming imperfect information: • Insurance (health, life, pensions) • Financial regulation • Consumer protection	Providing social insurance: • Redistributive pensions • Family allowances • Unemployment insurance
Activist Functions	Co-ordinating private activity: • Fostering markets • Cluster initiatives			Redistribution: • Asset redistribution

Source: World Bank, 1997: *The State in A Changing World. World Development Report 1997.*
        Oxford University Press. New York.

---

[3]   See generally World Bank, 1997: *The State in A Changing World. World Development Report 1997.* Oxford University Press. New York.

Within this context, the following sections discuss what the state should not do and what it must do.

What The State Should Not Do

This is often more important than what the state should do. Experience world-wide has pointed to some lessons concerning the effectiveness of state intervention in certain areas. For example it is unwise for states to:

- run enterprises: it is not uncommon for the state to operate utilities as public monopolies, e.g. telecommunications, electricity, urban water and waste management services. It is also not uncommon for such utilities to be inefficient and ineffective both in financial terms and in respect of delivering a reliable, quality service. Furthermore, they often act in practice so as to suppress innovation and promote monolithic, resource-wasteful policies that are unresponsive to endogenous or exogenous changes in market conditions. Privatisation of utilities yields significant efficiency gains and creates an altogether more open, innovative and responsive industry that is much more able to adapt to environmental and other pressures, but these gains for society can only be fully captured if there is effective regulatory oversight of the sector to monitor, *inter alia*, pricing structures and compliance with relevant legislation.

- over-manage markets: in general, governments intervene principally to "correct" market failures and to address issues of distributional equity. Typically such interventions have multiple objectives, e.g. seeking to combine economic, social, regional, industrial and other objectives in one intervention and are national in scale, thus eliminating diversity of solution and ignoring local differences. The result is frequently to produce perverse outcomes, to establish new rigidities which resist change, to frustrate innovation and to entrench inappropriate policy models such as the 'predict and provide' model that has generated wasteful public expenditure priorities in transport, housing and other areas of policy. In general, governments should only intervene in markets to improve market efficiency and should meet other legitimate policy objectives such as greater equity or high environmental standards directly through policies designed to achieve those objectives. Wherever possible, policy making should be devolved downward in order to achieve diversity of approach within a clear framework of national performance standards.

- provide open-ended economic support: subsidies and other economic support measures inhibit the internalisation of environmental and social costs of economic activities as reflected in the prices of goods and services. By lowering market prices of inputs such as fertiliser, water and energy, or by artificially raising revenues received by producers and industry, economic support measures can generate important environmental effects through encouraging higher levels of resource use and pollution, and wasteful production processes. Such support measures inevitably create dependent constituencies and substantial political rigidities, destroying both equity and efficiency alike. Responding to these effects may then require some form of policy intervention, often at additional cost. Decoupling support measures from production and input levels should be a high priority given the likely "win-win" economic and environmental benefits that would result. Subsidies are appropriate to achieve clearly targetted and time-limited step changes in performance in key areas.

Results from practical experience also suggest that state-driven, centralised policies are responsible for most of the worst examples of unsustainable development. Examples include:

- the Common Agriculture Policy in the European Union;
- electricity generation in the UK prior to privatisation;
- forest clearance in south-east Asia and Latin America;
- irrigation schemes in the former Soviet Union, with the case of the Aral Sea being the most well publicised.

This conclusion appears to hold whether the focus is on developed or developing countries or on market or socialist economies.

What the State Must Do

This can be divided into two areas, which are not mutually exclusive. First, meeting global responsibilities. Here the state has a vested interest on behalf of its citizens, the business sector and other stakeholders in contributing to the establishment of global 'rules of the game', such as in the area of trade and environment, investment (e.g. the current negotiation in the OECD of a Multi-lateral Agreement on Investment, which will be a free-standing international treaty open to OECD and non-OECD countries) and multi-lateral agreements on the environment. Moreover, many countries are members of regional economic arrangements, such as APEC, ASEAN, EU, NAFTA and MERCOSUR, which are developing 'rules of the game' that affect members' interests and responsibilities. Examples include the goal of APEC members to achieve free trade and investment in the Asia-Pacific region by 2020 and the agreement between the EU and 12 Mediterranean countries (Euromed) to establish free trade by 2010.

In addition, state's have a common interest in building "institutions for the earth". Although there have been positive developments, such as the establishment of the UN CSD to guide implementation of Agenda 21 and a "greening" of international finance institutions such as the World Bank, much remains to be done. The present set of international institutions and agreements covering the environment resemble a patchwork quilt with no coherent, co-ordinated focus or strategic vision. It is a perverse outcome of the Earth Summit that institutions to manage the global environment are now weaker and less well resourced than they were before. As noted in a recent OECD study[4], "In an era when environmental problems are increasingly supra-national, the limited capacity of existing international institutions to respond to these challenges is becoming more visible and acute" (page 126). A possible response suggested by some commentators is the establishment of a world environment organisation, similar in concept to the World Trade Organisation.

---

[4]   OECD, 1997: *The World in 2020. Towards a New Global Age*. OECD. Paris.

At a national level, the state has three clear tasks that it alone is well placed to carry out:

- it must invest in the capacity to manage the environment by ensuring that the scope and quality of environmental data is adequate to the complexity of the management task and that there is a robust legal framework in place together with properly resourced and professionally competent regulatory institutions to ensure compliance with policy goals;

- it must guarantee transparency by providing the legal and institutional framework, including free and unfettered mass media, to ensure the free flow of information among government, enterprises and the public about the environmental consequences of public and private activities and ensure that there are adequate opportunities for those affected by decisions to participate in their making. This inevitably means that it is essential for states to be vigorous in their efforts to suppress corrupt practices whose existence is inimicable to the transparency necessary for effective protection of the environment; and

- it must strengthen its own governance capacity in order to be able to achieve the level of integration of environment with other policies necessary to resolve policy conflicts.

4.0 Conclusion

We are not absolutely short of the resources, capital and technology to ensure a reasonable standard of living for twice the current world population without destroying the ecological foundation of the global economy. However, we do lack the capacity to link resources, capital and technology together in combinations which are sustainable. In a world in which economic and environmental interdependence between countries is strengthening, the globalisation of opportunity without an associated globalisation of responsibility will further erode that capacity.

EVOLVING PUBLIC-PRIVATE PARTNERSHIPS: GENERAL THEMES AND EXAMPLES FROM THE URBAN WATER SECTOR

Bradford Gentry and Lisa Fernandez
Yale Centre for Environmental Law and Policy, USA and the Yale/UNDP Program on Public-Private Partnerships for the Urban Environment

1.0   Introduction

Most of us prefer to stay on paths we know, sharing goals and work practices with people who think and act like us: governments working with governments, businesses with businesses, non-profit groups with non-profit groups.

Doing so in a globalising world, however, often means that we find it harder and harder to meet our core goals, whatever they may be -- economic development for governments, profits for businesses, or social development/environmental protection for NGOs. In addition, our separate, unco-ordinated actions often create redundancies and missed opportunities for optimizing the use of scarce resources (financial, social and environmental).

As a result, interaction with other sectors is increasingly necessary, and frequently difficult. Sometimes it results in conflict: protests, enforcement, disputed elections. Sometimes it leads to cooperative action: dialogue, joint planning, contractual and other arrangements.

The focus of this paper is on the growing effort to forge such co-operative relationships, the "evolving public-private partnerships." How do they start? Why are they happening? How are they organized? What are the conditions for success?

Some answers are provided from both general and specific perspectives. Given the huge variety of issues, actors and contexts affecting such relationships around the world, there are a virtually infinite number of possible responses. There are, however, general themes and organizing principles common to many of these efforts. Some of the major themes are described below. In addition, one set of issues -- delivering urban water services in developing countries -- is generating considerable interest in public-private sector co-operation. Cases from the urban water sector are therefore used here to illustrate how these general themes apply in one particular context.

2.0   The Catalyst for Public-Private Partnerships: A Widely Recognized Crisis

In most cases, it takes a crisis to stimulate radical changes in attitudes and encourage stakeholders to explore new working relationships. Some government agencies are concerned about being taken advantage of by private businesses, particularly multinational companies. Some businesses think that working with governments is a waste of time. Many NGOs believe that neither governments nor businesses can be trusted to meet priority needs.

It takes a special kind of crisis -- one which multiple groups acknowledge as affecting their core interests -- to forge lasting, co-operative relationships among public and private actors. It is not enough that governments, businesses or NGOs believe there is a crisis affecting their individual interests. Only when other groups recognize that the crisis also impairs their ability to achieve their individual goals does a basis for significant cooperation exist. Collective action to fulfill complementary individual needs which cannot be met alone is the foundation on which public-private partnerships are built.

One hopes that progress can also be made in the absence of a crisis. Longer-term planning, driven by a clear understanding of, and respect for, the needs of various parties should also lead to significant public-private co-operation. In practice, however, the inertia and reassurance of keeping to familiar paths is usually only broken by a pressing need to work together.

Individual "champions" of public-private cooperation also make a huge difference. These can be government officials, NGOs, business people, or citizens who through their personal drive make partnerships happen. In other cases, they are providers of services (such as water or waste treatment) who stand to profit from the partnership and, therefore, have clear commercial incentives to push for its formation.

One crisis that is generating numerous calls for public-private co-operation stems from the severe environmental problems facing many cities in the developing world. Viewed by some as the environmental issue of the 21st century, a brief description of its scope is provided in the next section.

The Urban Environmental Crisis

By the end of the century, and for the first time in history, more people will live in cities than in rural areas[1] . In developing countries, the urban population has tripled in the last three decades. With growing urbanization, poverty rates have risen and environmental hazards have increased, affecting human health, productivity and quality of life[2] .

In the poorest cities, indoor air pollution is the norm when soft coal and biomass fuels are used for heating and cooking. As cities grow (demographically and economically), industrial and vehicular emissions add to air pollution problems.

Inadequate supplies of clean water supply and wastewater treatment facilities raise acute concern. The UN estimates that "20 percent of the world's population lacks access to safe water

---

[1]   UN Habitat Conference, 1996: *An Urbanizing World: Global Report on Human Settlements.* United Nations.

[2]   World Bank, 1997: "Can the Environment Wait? Economic Growth and the Environment in East and Southeast Asia". Environment Department Draft Discussion Paper (July 22, 1997).

supply, while 50 percent lacks access to adequate sanitation."[3] Half the urban population in the southern hemisphere lacks piped water, while a quarter, or about 350 million people, lack any infrastructure of any kind for assuring water delivery. It is estimated that about twenty percent of city dwellers in developing countries obtain drinking water from vendors at very high prices, sometimes having to spend as much as a quarter of their income for it.

Sewerage service is even more limited throughout many urban areas and often absent in squatter settlements. Overall, perhaps a third of city dwellers in developing countries lack hygienic means of disposing human wastes; even more lack clean means for wastewater disposal[4]. For example, Jakarta has no central waterborne sewage system, and only 68 percent of the population is served by septic tanks. In Calcutta, only a third of the area in the urban core has sewerage, and poor maintenance has contributed to chronic annual flooding of the system.

The International Finance Corporation, a member of the World Bank Group, estimates that by 2025 one billion people could suffer water shortages unless governments adopt "radical change" to ensure supplies[5]. While governments recognize that water is becoming scarce, they balk at charging an economic price for it since it is so essential to human life. Instead they often choose to subsidize access. The results include massive water losses in the absence of any incentives for water conservation and few financial resources for expansion of clean water and sewerage services, particularly to poorer neighbourhoods.

The potential for collaborative public-private efforts in the water sector is to meet the challenges of providing broad, non-regressive access to supplies, protecting the environment, and preventing abuses of monopoly distribution rights[6]. The next section of this paper examines the reasons why public and private parties are taking joint responsibility for financing and providing services -- such as water supplies -- in developing country cities.

3.0   Public-Private Sector Partnerships: "Win-Win" Opportunities to Meet Shared Needs

The urban environmental crisis in developing countries is just one of a number of problems generating increased calls for public-private co-operation; economic regeneration, retraining workers in transition, affordable housing are also important policy challenges. Given the historic difficulties public and private actors face in working together, why the push to partnerships?

---

[3] UN Secretary General, 1997: "Comprehensive Assessment of Freshwater Resources of the World" (February 1997). See also Barham, J., 1997: "How to Sell the World's Water Industry" in The Financial Times (October 2, 1997).

[4] UN Habitat Conference, 1996: see Footnote 1.

[5] Duff, D., International Finance Corporation quoted in Barham, J., 1997: see Footnote 3. Also, Swarzberg, T., 1997: "World Water. The World's Freshwater Supplies: The Crunch is Here" in International Herald Tribune (September 30, 1997).

[6] World Bank, 1996: *Frontiers of the Public-Private Interface in East Asia's Infrastructure.* Proceedings of the Ministerial Level International Conference on Infrastructure Development. Jakarta, Indonesia. September 2-4, 1996.

The primary reason is that neither the public nor private sector can meet their respective needs acting alone. State domination of the economy and public services has not worked. Unfettered pursuit of individual gain in the market leads to under-investment in the human and social capital necessary for businesses to thrive.

In addition, co-operation increases the chances for optimizing system resources. Financial resources and technical know-how are limited. Leveraging off others' complementary activities may increase their impact. Social and environmental resources are also increasingly stretched. Responding to crises by focusing on optimizing resource use -- across the public and private sectors -- should increase the effectiveness and efficiency of the strategies chosen.

Efforts to build on these opportunities are also consistent with several broader trends, including:

- Globalisation of the world economy, including the shift from foreign aid to private capital as the engine of economic growth for large parts of the developing world[7] ;

- Shrinking public sector budgets at a time when increasing amounts of private capital are potentially available;

- Devolution of government authority from national to regional/local authorities and the corresponding need to increase their capacity to fulfill the new responsibilities; and

- Increasing amounts of information becoming available to greater numbers of people through the media, the internet and global commerce.

All of these trends underscore the needs -- and opportunities -- for increased efforts to cooperate in the application of public and private resources to address shared concerns.

This is not to say that public-private co-operation will always be effective or that it should always be sought. While many of the goals of governments and businesses overlap, their core objectives are different, for example, promoting social versus shareholder wealth. Their core roles are also different. While many governments are moving from being the provider to the enabler and regulator of services[8] , private interests are expanding their role as provider of basic services, but only where there is a potential for profit.

Clarity in the allocation of roles and identification of core objectives is critical to successful public-private co-operation. Such efforts already face many obstacles. For example, failure to specify who is to do what and perceptions of impropriety are sure ways to terminate or damage severely any public-private partnerships.

---

[7] Schmidheiny, S. and Gentry, B.S., 1997: "Privately Financed Sustainable Development" in *Thinking Ecologically: Building the Next Generation of Environmental Policy.* Yale University Press. New Haven.

[8] See generally World Bank, 1997: *World Development Report 1997: The State in a Changing World.* Oxford University Press. New York.

How these themes are reflected in the urban water sector are described below.

Need for Joint Solutions to Urban Environmental Problems

The need for partnerships between the public and private sectors in addressing urban environmental problems rests on three major factors.

First, governments can no longer go it alone. The explosive growth of cities in the developing world has led to crises in both the social and environmental dimensions. On the social front, municipal governments have trouble maintaining existing infrastructure, much less responding adequately to growing demand in areas of uncontrolled expansion. This situation leads to an increasingly inequitable pattern in the provision of public services: the poorest residents at the urban fringe have the least access to safe water, solid waste collection, or electricity. On the environmental front, the expansion of cities without an accompanying upgrading of infrastructure turns environmental "goods" like clean water and air into environmental "bads", such as dirty water, polluted air. Natural resource assets become instead sinks not only for human and industrial waste, but also for human potential.

Most developing country governments, particularly those in cities, lack the resources and capacity to address these crises on their own. They need funds to expand services or buy new technology. The costs of upgrading water infrastructure in a single city range up to $10 billion; for an entire country like Poland, this may cost up to $40 billion[9] . They need information to optimize system resources. Increasingly, they are looking to the private sector -- both the "for-profit" and "not-for-profit" -- to help.

Second, the goals of the public and private sectors increasingly overlap in the urban environmental arena, particularly in developing and rapidly industrialising countries. Demands for access to clean drinking water and treatment of wastewater are increasingly shared by public and private actors in the urban sector. Acknowledgment of those shared needs provides a basis for increased public-private sector co-operation, examples of which provide the context for much of the rest of this paper.

The vocabulary differs, but the public and private sectors share many goals. Both seek to raise general standards of living: businesses so that more people can afford their products, governments to alleviate poverty. They are also seeking to build more links at the local level, particularly in "emerging markets": businesses to support market growth, governments (and multilateral development agencies) to promote social development and a fertile exchange of cost-effective "best practices". These shared goals of increasing wealth and communication around the globe, in the face of scarce resources, also translate into a common focus on efficient collaboration to promote quality environments which are also successful cities and dynamic market economies.

To date, private capital investments in public works have been very limited. This is because few projects, particularly in the lowest income countries, can meet the rigorous financial and

---

[9]   Swarzberg, T., 1997: see Footnote 5. Also, Bobinski, C., 1997: "Poland Faces Big Bill to Bring Water Supply to EU Standard" in The Financial Times (October 6, 1997).

risk criteria private investors require[10] . According to the UN, however, private investor interest is growing, as governments become more adept at embracing private sector needs and motivations when seeking business participation in infrastructure services. In 1996, about 250 infrastructure projects in the southern hemisphere were considered for private sector financing, 72 of which were in low income countries[11] . In particular, the water sector is a relative newcomer to privatization: only five percent of financing for water worldwide comes from private sources[12] . Interest and opportunities are growing, however.

Third, public-private sector co-operation can help ensure that benefits are maximized at lowest cost and distributed evenly. In addition to money, the private sector brings efficiency (in production, service provision and decision-making), financial know-how, consumer choice, and technical expertise to bear on such co-operative arrangements[13] . The private sector's emphasis on "time is money" and returns-driven agendas also support focused, performance-oriented project management[14].

Governments also contribute a number of critical skills. They include: public accountability (to help ensure equitable distribution of benefits); local knowledge; legal frameworks; and an enabling environment. In addition, government oversight and regulation, particularly of monopoly services like water supply, is necessary to protect consumers. In Argentina, effective regulator oversight increased and made more equitable the distribution of gains from privatization. When regulation was not effective, overall gains were fewer and unevenly distributed such that the poorest income classes suffered at the expense the wealthy[15] .

Public-private partnerships can be organized in many different ways. Some of the major options are described in the next section.

---

[10] See generally Gentry, B.S, 1996: "Breaking the Bottlenecks to Private Participation in East Asian Infrastructure: Environmental and Resettlement Issues" in World Bank, 1996: *Frontiers of the Public-Private Interface in East Asia's Infrastructure.* Proceedings of the Ministerial Level International Conference on Infrastructure Development. Jakarta, Indonesia. September 2-4, 1996.

[11] UN Habitat Conference, 1996: see Footnote 1.

[12] Frenchman, M., 1997: "World Water. First Priority: Finding the Funding" in International Herald Tribune (September 30, 1997).

[13] Faulkner, J.H., 1997: "Engaging the Private Sector Through Public-Private Partnerships" in *Bridges to Sustainability: Business and Government Working Together for a Better Environment.* A Contribution of the Yale/UNDP Program on Public Private Partnerships to the UN General Assembly Special Session "Earth Summit+5". Bulletin 101, Yale School of Forestry and Environmental Studies (July 1997).

[14] Livingston, N., 1997: Sustainable Project Management. Personal communication, October 1997.

[15] Chisari, O., Estache, A. and Romero, C., 1997: Winners and Losers from Utility Privatization in Argentina: Lessons from a General Equilibrium Model. Policy Research Working Paper No. 1824 (September 1997). World Bank, Economic Development Institute, Regulatory Reform and Private Enterprise Division. Washington D.C.

4.0   Organising Public-Private Partnerships: Parties, Roles and Forms

When thinking about how public-private partnerships are organized it is critical to consider their component parts, namely:

- the *parties* who are potential participants and their needs;

- the multiple *roles* those parties may play as part of the partnership; and

- the spectrum of *forms* the partnership might take.

Each of these is discussed below, both generally and using examples from the urban water sector.

Parties: Possible Participants and Their Needs

Many different parties have a possible interest in forming partnerships, some of whom fall outside the strict confines of the "public sector" or the "private sector."

- Governments: It is important to recognize that government, commonly identified as the prime interested party, is not monolithic. First, government entities at different levels are all potential participants, from local municipal offices, to regional, state or provincial administrations, to national or federal secretariats. Second, each of these levels includes individuals with often conflicting agendas - elected officials, civil servants, workers in the government operation facing greater private involvement. These individuals will make or break any effort at co-operation. For example, private participation in infrastructure services is usually considered a threat by public employees, who assume that their jobs are at stake. Addressing their legitimate concerns without sacrificing the efficiency gains private participation promises is one of the delicate balancing acts government plays in partnership arrangements.

- Businesses. Although more public-private partnerships may be emerging because of globalisation, partnerships always happen in a particular place, i.e. they are locally driven. Multinational companies are commonly thought of as potential parties for infrastructure services because of their financial resources and access to loans. Local firms may not have the financial backing or the economic wealth, but their long standing ties to the customer base and the labor force make them essential participants in successful partnerships.

  Businesses who participate in the partnership expect to make a reasonable profit, either as the user or provider of the service. Difficulties can arise where this goal is insufficiently acknowledged or honoured by public participants.

- NGOs. The not-for-profit community is a critical part of the private sector, playing a myriad of roles both in facilitating and running partnerships. Freed of the need to make a profit, civic groups and institutions play important roles in supporting partnerships at various levels. Sophisticated NGOs with ties to local elites, as well as international

105

environmental and charity groups, can be ideal champions for involving the wealthy and the powerful on a particular issue. Such groups can also be articulate advocates vis-à-vis the media. Smaller scale and usually more locally based community development organizations play critical roles as advocates for disadvantaged groups, in particular supporting small-scale infrastructure projects that are direly needed but largely ignored by larger businesses. In order to capture their involvement, the needs of the NGO community must also be met: the partnership must advance their cause, be it enfranchising the poor or protecting the integrity of a local ecosystem.

Roles: Core Functions In The Successful Provision of Services

Where the purpose of the partnership is to address a crisis by providing missing services, there are three major roles to be played: provider; user; and regulator of the services. Each of the parties identified above can undertake any of these roles in any particular case. The key is clarity in the allocation and definition of these roles, along with adequate dialogue to ensure that the needs of the different parties are met.

- Providers. These are the parties who actually supply the desired service, e.g. housing, training, waste collection. They will do so if they have access to the necessary resources (financial and otherwise) and can provide the service in a manner that meets their core needs. Access to financial resources depends, in large part, on the strength of the partnership structure and the predictability of its future performance. Meeting core needs varies with the party providing the service: for businesses it is a reasonable expectation of profit, for NGOs it is meeting their social or environmental objectives.

- Users. These are the parties who increasingly pay for the services being provided. While more broadly based government revenues have traditionally been used in many cases, with the reductions in government finance, users are more frequently being asked to bear the full cost of the service. Many will be willing to do so, but only as long as the quality of the service supplied is acceptable. If it is not, serious problems will develop (as illustrated by the IWK case described below). For others who are willing but not able to pay the full costs, other forms of income support are increasingly being considered instead of reduced user fees.

- Regulators. Where there are multiple providers of a service, customer demand and other market forces are likely to ensure that the service price and quality is acceptable. In these situations, users function as the major regulators of price and quality. Where there are monopoly or only a small number of providers, more extensive, governmental regulatory structures are needed to address market failures on price and quality. Generally, this role is undertaken by the public sector, but NGOs, citizens, users and others may well be involved. Exercising this regulatory function in a manner which enhances the predictability of financial performance, rather than increasing the uncertainty, is key to the provider's ability to obtain the necessary resources.

Forms: Types of "Public-Private Partnerships" That Are Evolving

There is no single definition of the term "public-private partnership." As shown in Figure 1, the term should be viewed as describing a spectrum of possible relationships between public and private actors for the co-operative provision of services. There is a virtually infinite number of individual points on that spectrum, with a multiplicity of forms for co-operation continually emerging.

The only essential element is some degree of private participation in the provision of traditionally public-domain services. As Haarmeyer and Mody put it in their most useful summary of experience in the water sector, "The different arrangements represent a continuum of allocations of risks and responsibilities between the public and private sector. Increasing private sector responsibility is associated with increasing government commitment and assumption of regulatory risk."[16]

Choosing among these different forms depends upon a number of issues, including:

- the degree of control desired by the government;

- the government's capacity to provide the desired services;

- the capacity of private parties to provide the services;

- the legal frameworks for private investment and regulatory oversight; and

- the availability of financial resources from public or private sources.

The following section uses examples from the urban water sector to illustrate how some of these forms have been applied in a specific context.

5.0   Public-Private Partnerships In The Urban Water Sector

Urban water issues generate an increasing number of co-operative relationships, taking a wide variety of forms. The following cases are not presented as a march along the spectrum in Figure 1. Rather, they follow a rough historical progression of the types of structures that are used to expand private involvement in water services: dialogue and joint planning; management and operating contracts; build-operate-transfer or "BOTs"; concessions; joint ventures; and NGO-led provision of basic services.

---

[16]   Haarmeyer, D. and Mody, A., 1997: Tapping the Private Sector: Reducing Risk to Attract
Expertise and Capital to Water and Sanitation. Draft Report (April 1997). World Bank,
Project Finance and Guarantees Division. See also Brook Cowan, P.J., 1997: "The Private
Sector in Water and Sanitation: How to Get Started" in *Public Policy for the Private Sector*.
World Bank. Washington D.C.

Figure 1: Spectrum of Possible Relationships Between Public and Private Service Providers

Note: Major headings are provided for illustration only; many other forms are continually evolving

Fully Public Sector:	Informal Cooperation:	"Petite" Privatization:	"Traditional" Public Contracting:	"Core" Public-Private Partnerships:	Public Financial Support:	"Grande" Privatization:	Informal Cooperation:	*Fully Private Sector:*
protests	dialogue joint planning	operate manage	study design build	co-shareholding co-ownership co-responsibility	loans equity insurance grants	"BOT" concession sale	joint planning dialogue	*enforcement*

—————— Contractual Arrangements ——————

—————— Broadest Definition of "Public-Private Partnerships" ——————

Dialogue and Joint Planning

The lack of access to clean water and the increasing pollution of surface waters creates crises leading to co-operative action. While coercive responses are often appropriate -- such as protests against poor government services or enforcement against polluters -- the first steps in co-operative relationships are dialogue on the nature of the problem and joint planning for its solution.

At a minimum, this involves dialogue over a period of time, enabling the different groups to determine where they share needs and concerns. Joint planning may also occur where different parties consider applying their individual resources in a manner co-ordinated with others' efforts. Doing so increases the chances that application of the total pool of available resources will be optimized to everyone's benefit. This may include optimizing technical solutions, as well as the pricing or distribution of services.

The broader the dialogue, the greater the acceptance of the solution, but also the greater the time and resources necessary to put it in place. Deciding where the appropriate balance lies is extremely difficult, and will largely be determined by the individual context. Box 1 describes the case of Ilo, Peru where major public protests eventually led to broadly based dialogue and joint planning of widely accepted, effective solutions.

Moving from dialogue to effective implementation can be a major hurdle. Having people express an interest in a problem is one thing, having them put money and time into its solution is another. Box 2 summarises the case of Juarez, Mexico, where implementation of a regional solution has been delayed for a variety of reasons.

Box 1: Ilo, Peru: Out of crisis, dialogue and planning, then clean-up and a commitment to coherent urban growth[17]

Since the 1950s, the population of Ilo, a coastal city in southern Peru, has grown nearly 20-fold, to about 70,000 people. Lack of urban planning, in-migration and industrialization led to uncontrolled and chaotic development. Traditional fishing activities became severely depleted as a result of seawater contamination from local industry. Industry also controlled many sources of drinking and irrigation water, curtailing their use by the public. Local mines felt threatened by the growth in population that gradually spilled over onto their land. Over time, a high level of animosity developed between the residents of the town and the largest industrial concern, Southern Peru Ltd.

In the late 1980s, an Environmental Management Committee was set up to diffuse this tension and develop a comprehensive plan to solve the problems. The committee included representatives of Southern Peru Ltd., the fishing industry, universities, municipal officials, residents, and the health department.

One of the first aims of the Committee was to establish clear pollution norms. Working with all stakeholders, the committee was able to obtain central government acceptance of its norms, as well as to persuade local industry to undertake environmental clean up. In return, community members agreed to channel their protests to the municipal authorities, and both sides agreed to conduct negotiations with transparency and pragmatism.

The negotiation process was slow and full of obstacles. However, by acknowledging that all the parties were responsible for the solution, the obstacles were slowly overcome and a number of solutions proposed. The two most important were:

- an Environmental Plan for Southern Peru Ltd., including a commitment by the company to invest $100 million in environmental improvements in partnership with the government. This included the development of: two industrial and urban waste water plants; a refuse disposal site and sanitary landfill; a reforestation program for the region; and other controls to mitigate sea pollution.

- an Urban Development Commission, appointed to reorganize Ilo's General Plan along the following lines: redesignating those lands subject to mining claims; restructuring the urban space through consolidation of railway tracks and development of pedestrian crossings; and building parks and playgrounds.

One of the major successes of this partnership has been the development of a vision for the future of the city that takes into account the rights of all stakeholders. The Ilo case shows that a climate of confrontation can stimulate constructive solutions if there is frank recognition of different interests and a willingness to accept responsibility.

---

[17]   Badshah, A., 1997: Asia Pacific Cities Forum, Personal communication, October 15, 1997. Additional material from a presentation prepared by the Ilo city government and presented on its behalf at the Conference "Business and Municipality: New Partnerships for the 21st Century", Bremen, Germany, March 1997.

Box 2: Juarez, Mexico: Dialogue, then joint commitments, then delays due to limited municipal capacity and a rapid fall in the country's economy[18]

In 1991, a public-private task force was formed with Mexican and U.S. involvement to consider building wastewater treatment facilities to handle the 30 million pounds of raw sewage generated in Juarez each day. By the following year, financing was tentatively arranged under which the Mexican federal environmental authority and a private contractor would split the $US70 million cost of the proposed plants. However, ground was never broken for construction and to this day Juarez' sewage goes untreated.

A variety of hurdles have impeded implementation of the agreement. Some have focused on reopening consideration of the project structure. Others concern whether the core needs of the involved parties are likely to be met. Major issues include shifting economic policies in Mexico, including mandated privatization of water treatment infrastructure; an expanded array of stakeholders and new potential sources of financing with the establishment of the Border Environmental Commission and the North American Development Bank under NAFTA; Mexico's peso crisis (which raised the cost of capital); the absence of institutional capacity at the municipal level to guarantee returns to private parties; and poorly mediated conflicts of interest and cultural differences between private and public sector stakeholders, as well as between U.S. and Mexican interests.

Lessons

The cases profiled above, one successful, one stalled, show how important it is to identify solutions that meet the needs of the major interested parties. In the case of Ilo, this was done by an early commitment on the part of the stakeholders to transparency in the negotiating process. This also helped stimulate commitment by the participants in making the process work and reaching a solution. In Juarez, the stumbling blocks were only made larger by what was perceived as a lack of political will on the part of the municipality to take into account the profit motive stimulating private stakeholder investment.

The Ilo case also illustrates how early, transparent and informal communication among stakeholders can contribute to a good outcome. Although the negotiating process grew more formal over time, it was rooted in the fact that all parties to the agreement had been clear about their needs and motivations from the beginning. The Ilo case evolved into a contractual relationship to develop environmental infrastructure, a much more formal type of partnership than anyone probably envisioned in the beginning when the simple process of dialogue started.

All of the cases described in the rest of this section also started with some degree of dialogue and joint planning, the amount depending on the scope of the relationship contemplated. Where relatively straightforward operating and management contracts or one-off treatment works are involved (such as in the Mexico City or Izmit, Turkey examples presented here), extremely broad participation may be less necessary in order to achieve progress quickly. Where more comprehensive solutions are

---

[18]   Kapur, N. and Reynolds, A., 1998: "Waste Water: The Case of Juarez, Mexico" in Gentry, B.S. (ed.), 1998: *Private Capital Flows and the Environment in Latin America*. Edward Elgar Publishing Inc. Aldershot, U.K.

contemplated (such as in Buenos Aires, Malaysia or Ethiopia examples noted below), much more extensive discussions will need to occur over a longer period of time. Where contracts are signed and money invested before full dialogue is completed, renegotiation of legal obligations may well be required.

Operation and Management Contracts

If governments are wary of giving up too much control over water services, they may enter into operating and management contracts with private providers. Generally for short terms (five to seven years), they should allow the government to obtain some improvements in performance and efficiency, as well as a more complete understanding of their water problems. They do not, however, generate significant investments of private capital in the system.

Many people view such contracts as a relatively low-risk first step for expanding the role of the private sector. Box 3 describes the case of Mexico City where this approach has been applied.

Box 3: Mexico City, Mexico: Phasing in private sector management (rehabilitate, operate, transfer)[19]

The water and sewerage systems in Mexico City are well developed, but face many operating challenges. The aquifer that supplies water to Mexico City is overused. The drinking water distribution network suffers from major leakages, with losses of up to 30 percent. Less than half of the water consumed by the system is billed, and only 70 percent of bills are paid. In 1997, an operating deficit of 2.6 million pesos was expected.

In developing responses, the government's upfront capital needs were quite limited, given that the existing network reaches 98 percent of the population for drinking water and 94 percent for sewerage. On the other hand, its needs for technical and commercial expertise in water operations were great and could be provided by private companies. Phasing in private management of the system would also alleviate some of the political problems anticipated in efforts to increase the rate of fee collections from users.

As a result, the government chose to enter into a phased program of contracts with the private sector. First, competition was built in by dividing the city into four zones and issuing four tenders. The lowest price for performing the tasks in each phase won the contracts, which were awarded to four different companies for 10 year terms in October 1993. Second, each contract anticipated three phases of work. Phases 1 and 2 involve identifying customers, as well as designing and implementing a more effective billing system. The government is to pay the contractors directly on a simple fee-for-service basis for this work. In Phase 3 (not necessarily performed after Phase 1 and 2 depending on the local system needs), the principal task is to make improvements in the physical distribution system. In this phase, contractors' compensation is tied to revenue earned (fees collected from customers).

The fall of the peso and a dispute from a losing bidder caused delays in commissioning the work. Still, installation of water meters was expected to be completed by the end of 1997, an important step in discouraging excess consumption. A leak detection program has also been initiated to help with bill collection and reduce water losses by a third or more.

Lessons

Operation and management contracts have great potential for reducing water losses through better system operation and increasing revenues by improving collection systems. They also leave the government in charge of many of the more difficult political issues: the fee imposed for water services and ownership of the underlying assets.

Those same strengths, however, also define the limits of such contracts: they do not involve significant infusions of private capital, nor do they create a base from which to optimize the entire water systems. As described in the following sections, more extensive contractual arrangements are necessary for these initiatives to occur[20] .

---

[19] Haarmeyer, D. and Mody, A., 1997: see Footnote 16.

[20] See generally "A Wave of Privatization" in Infrastructure Finance (June 1997).

Build-Operate-Transfer (BOT)

BOTs are an effective way to bring private money into the construction of new water treatment facilities or substantially renovate existing ones. Closest to the model used for new power plants, such contracts require the private operators to:

- obtain the money necessary to build the plant;
- operate the plant so as to meet specified performance standards for a set period of time; and
- transfer the plant to the government at the end of the contract period.

In return, the government agrees to buy all of the output from the plant for a price calculated to repay the operator's costs and generate a reasonable profit. One example of such an arrangement is in Izmit, Turkey, as described in Box 4.

Since BOTs generally involve only one facility, they do not improve performance or efficiencies in other parts of the system (beyond the additional supply or treatment capacity they provide). They can, however, provide a platform for increasing local capacity to operate water facilities. One example of this approach from South Africa is described in Box 5.

Box 4: Izmit, Turkey: Host country support makes a difference in attracting private capital[21]

Seven years of negotiation led, in 1995, to the signing of a $933 million BOT contract for construction of a new drinking water plant to serve the 1.2 million residents of Izmit, a coastal town southeast of Istanbul. Thames Water of Britain is the lead investor in the consortium to build and operate the plant, which is destined to revert to the state 15 years after operations begin.

The largest privately financed water supply project in the world, Izmit is unique because of its innovative financing structure. First, there is substantial local participation. Thames Water has agreed to work with two local Turkish contractors who share in 70 percent of the equity. Furthermore, the municipality owns 15 percent of the project. Second, and perhaps the most critical aspect of the Izmit financing, the Turkish central government is guaranteeing 85 percent repayment of construction costs. This guarantee opened the doors to international finance in the face of concerns over "political risks" in Turkey. The Japanese banks Mitsui and Sumitomo took another 15 percent of the equity and arranged for $180 million in debt, repayable in untied aid. Financing arrangements were also supported by the export credit agencies in Britain, France, and Japan who covered political and commercial risk and divided up the debt financing.

---

[21] Swarzberg, T., 1997: see Footnote 5; Frenchman, M., 1997: see Footnote 12; Haarmeyer, D. and Mody, A., 1997: see Footnote 16.

The Izmit agreement is a "take-or-pay" type obligating the city to pay for a minimum amount and a maximum amount of water delivered by the project company. This deal ensures the concessionaire the ability to pay back the project's debt, and if the municipality were to default, lenders have recourse to the Turkish government.

Box 5: South Africa: Integrating training into BOT agreements[22]

A new variant on BOT arrangements is "Build-Operate-Train-Transfer" (BOTT). Although not yet widely applied, this approach is designed to help build local capacity to operate the new facilities at the time of transfer. For example, the government of South Africa has sought proposals for new rural water systems, including a requirement that local residents be trained on how to run the system once it is built. Implementation of the training requirement is to be monitored by South Africa's Department of Water Affairs.

This particular arrangement is somewhat simplified in relation to classic BOT models because substantial private investment is not sought, it is a simple government procurement contract. Mixed shareholdings are also required in the operating company, including black empowerment groups. These features are intended to build local acceptance and experience in commercialization of water infrastructure.

Lessons

Izmit is the first water sector BOT agreement in Turkey and one of the first in the world. The BOT model has been highly touted for water projects because it is closest to that used to build new power plants in many developing countries. Thus, potential financial partners and operators have less of a learning curve to climb in structuring such transactions. One key feature of BOT agreements is that market and credit risks are minimized because the government is the only customer, eliminating the risk of insufficient demand and reducing concerns over ability to pay.

The national government's guarantee of the Izmit project, while central to its financing, does raise concerns in many quarters that these are not sufficiently "private" projects, that they are ultimately another call on general government revenues. Private investor's concerns over political risk need to be allayed, however, if not by guarantees, then by project structures which are predictable and can be relied upon when forecasting financial returns.

The facility-specific focus of BOTs limits their ability to help optimize system resources or efficiencies. In order to capture these gains, concessions have been the preferred structure.

Concessions

Concessions combine the scope of management contracts with the private investment accompanying BOTs. In essence, the government cedes control over the delivery of water services in a specified region to a private operating company. The operator is responsible for obtaining the money to

---

[22]   Hargreaves, J., 1997: Northumbrian Lyonnaise des Eaux, personal communication, October 23, 1997.

upgrade and expand the system, and for meeting specified performance standards. In return, the operator collects fees directly from the system customers.

The government's role is fundamentally changed in nature, but not decreased in importance. It moves from being the provider of the service to the regulator of its price and quality. This is a particularly critical role in the water sector, given that water is a public good and its delivery systems are natural monopolies[23]. Governments' new, critical role as regulator of water services requires substantial changes in the way they have worked in the water sector and the acquisition of substantial new capacities.

Large-scale water concessions are politically controversial and difficult to organize. One example of a concession which has worked is in Buenos Aires, Argentina (Box 6).

---

[23]   World Bank, 1997: see Footnote 8.

Box 6: Aguas Argentinas, Buenos Aires: Great progress, but unclear requirements and missed opportunities for system optimization[24]

As part of Argentina's extensive privatization program in the early 1990's, control over Buenos Aires' water and sewage system was awarded to Aguas Argentinas ("AA"), a consortium led by the French company Lyonnaise des Eaux. In order to win the bid, AA offered the greatest reduction in then existing water tariffs. It also agreed to a 30 year investment plan of US$4 billion to connect 100% of the population in the concession area to drinking water and 90% to sewerage. Funding for the investment program came from a euro-commercial paper offering, IFC syndicated loans and partly from commercial banks.

Since winning the concession, AA has connected over half a million new residents to drinking water and 300,000 people to the sewerage system. Drinking water supplies have grown and quality has improved. Increased efficiency has led to economic and environmental benefits through the reduced use of chemicals. Commercial incentives have led AA to conduct water quality sampling more frequently than required by regulation and to re-examine how to address the difficult issue of wastewater treatment.

Argentina's overlapping authorities to regulate environmental matters have led to some confusion. It is unclear whether AA is subject only to the regulatory structure authorizing the concession, including environmental standards enforced by a specially created regulatory body, or also to separate, conflicting legislation enforced by the national environment ministry as well as provincial and municipal authorities. Efforts are on-going to clarify the applicable rules so that the concessionaire can operate in a more certain regulatory climate and proceed on projects that have been delayed due to the confusion over authority.

In addition, opportunities to optimize the wastewater treatment system were missed during the privatization process. Because of the speed with which the government decided to proceed, it required bidders to agree to construct several specific wastewater collection and treatment facilities identified in prior government planning documents. Serious questions have been raised about whether these specific facilities are the most cost-effective way to address the wastewater issues facing the city. Pursuit of different, more efficient investment plans led to the disqualification of one bidder and efforts to renegotiate the concession by the winning bidder.

---

[24] Gentry, B.S., 1998: "Argentina: Buenos Aires Water and Sewerage" in Gentry, B.S. (ed.), 1998: *Private Capital Flows and the Environment in Latin America.* Edward Elgar Publishing Inc. Aldershot, U.K.

Water concessions do not necessarily need to be for combined water and sewerage systems, or even on a municipal level, although these are the usual models. One example of a different approach is provided by the IWK concession in Malaysia (Box 7).

Box 7: Indah Water Konsortium (IWK), Malaysia: Technically innovative, but hampered by a lack of public acceptance[25]

In the late 1980's and early 1990's, the Malaysian government became increasingly concerned about environmental problems caused by sewage discharges and the lack of investment by local authorities in sewage collection or treatment. At the same time, the country was moving aggressively to privatize many government operations in an effort to reduce the size of government, increase efficiency, and increase the shareholdings of native Malays.

In response, a number of private companies formed IWK to offer the government a private, national solution to the sewerage problem. Key aspects of IWK's proposal were to reduce capital costs by using smaller, decentralized systems and to have more populous areas help underwrite the costs of providing sewage services in more rural districts.

Consistent with its practice of encouraging unsolicited bids, the government rewarded this private initiative with the grant of exclusive negotiating rights for a national sewerage concession. After a more detailed study of the concept by IWK and preparation of the contractual and regulatory framework, the concession was awarded in December 1993.

Under the concession, IWK is to take over the sewerage operations of the 144 local authorities in Malaysia. It is expected to invest approximately US$2.4 billion renovating, upgrading and adding new sewage collection and treatment facilities, in order to bring them into compliance with existing and future Malaysian effluent discharge standards. Part of this investment program is funded by a soft loan from the government. Other financing is expected to come from shareholder equity, operating revenues and local sources of private capital sources. A newly created office of the Director-General of Sewerage Services (DGSS) is responsible for ensuring that IWK both meets the terms of the concession agreement and earns a return on investment which falls into a specified range.

IWK's work under the concession has been dogged by problems since the beginning. First, there has been a continuing series of challenges to its fees. Commercial users in particular felt that they were being subjected to substantially increased fees for sewerage services they were not using or receiving. Second, IWK's relationship with the individual Malaysian states faces many challenges, ranging from the need to rely on state water companies to collect IWK's new sewerage fee to obtaining rights to land for the new facilities. These problems have been exacerbated by the manner in which the concession was awarded (without public bidding) and its structure (separating water supply from wastewater treatment, and doing so on a national rather than a regional or watershed basis).

---

[25] Gentry, B.S., 1996: Privatization, Foreign Investment and the Environment: Case Studies of Large Scale Privatizations with Foreign Participation. World Bank Environment Department Research Paper. July 1996.

Lessons

The AA concession has been successful in improving water services and reducing fees. The issues of regulatory structures and system optimization remain to be fully addressed, however. Although IWK had more scope to optimize delivery systems, the unsolicited bid process exacerbated political issues and may have masked broader project structuring risks in the concessionaire's plan.

In essence, both concessions have suffered -- to widely varying degrees -- from a failure to undertake sufficient dialogue and joint planning in advance of entering into binding contractual commitments. In the case of AA, an optimal approach would have been to involve more government departments in the design of the regulatory structure and to give the bidders more flexibility in designing systems for meeting wastewater discharge requirements. Given the severe fiscal and service crises facing the Argentine government at that time, however, it made sense to move more swiftly than the ideal situation would have allowed. In the case of IWK, pilot testing of the proposed concession with users, states and other water companies may have helped the government identify and address in advance the problems now plaguing the system.

Concerning public procurement, as noted in Figure 1 there is a long history of governments contracting with private firms for studies, facility design and construction services. Formal procedures for awarding such contracts have developed over the years to help governments obtain the best price possible and to protect against discriminatory treatment of bidders. In most cases, bids are sought based on highly detailed project specifications developed by governments and their consultants. Winners are determined based on their experience and the price they offer for delivering the specified services, as was done in the case of AA.

AA also demonstrates the difficulties of applying the traditional approach when awarding contracts for systems that are likely to evolve over a period of 25 years or longer. No one can predict in advance with the level of certainty applied in traditional public sector bid specifications the most efficient and effective ways to provide the desired service over that period of time. In addition, private operators, not government officials or consultants, are more likely to generate the most cost-effective alternatives for delivering such services. As such, governments are better served by concentrating on specifying performance standards, rather than on how those standards should be met. This means that governments must develop the capacity to evaluate and select among the different methods proposed for achieving those standards. In addition, concession contracts should anticipate and provide for the evolution of capital investment programs over time. A number of ways to do this are being explored, ranging from having bidders offer a total amount of investment they are willing to make based upon a specified water fee without specifying how the total investment will be allocated, to contractual provisions for revision of capital investment programs throughout the term.

Finally, it should be noted that most of the water concessions to date have been carried out at the national level: Buenos Aires, Malaysia, Manila, Jakarta. In part this may be due to the greater size, and hence financial strength, of these concessions. It may also be due to the fact that they are being driven by national government leaders as part of their broader privatization efforts.

How this experience affects efforts to devolve national governmental responsibilities to local and regional authorities remains to be seen. Many regional and municipal officials are less active supporters of privatization. They have strong ties to public sector workers. Their water systems are smaller, and hence the potential base for revenues is small as well.

119

At the same time, smaller cities often have the most acute need for improved water services along with the fewest resources, financial and technical. Designing and implementing innovative approaches to increase private sector involvement in delivering environmental services at the sub-national level is urgent. Amalgamating service areas may be one way to achieve economies of scale. Bringing public and private actors together as co-owners of water companies may be another, as discussed in the next section.

"Core" Public-Private Partnerships: Co-shareholding, Ownership and Responsibility

What degree of control should governments have over water services? This is the question that plagues many efforts to increase the private sector role in water. One the one hand and in many cases, full governmental control has led to poor service from inefficient systems. On the other hand, as a monopoly business filling a critical human need, full private control, while most economically "efficient," is often politically unacceptable.

Management contracts keep the government in control whereas concessions change the government role to arm's-length regulator. Joint ventures and mixed capital companies offer a middle position. They provide a vehicle for "true" public-private partnerships in which governments, businesses, NGOs and others can pool their resources and generate shared "returns" by solving local water issues[26]. In these cases, the government is the ultimate regulator, but it also is an active shareholder in the operating company. From that position, it may share in the operating company's profits and help ensure the wider political acceptability of its efforts. One example of such an approach in Cartagena, Colombia is described in Box 8.

---

[26] See generally Faulkner, J.H., 1997: see Footnote 13.

Lessons

Given the political sensitivity surrounding water, such joint ventures offer attractive possibilities for combining local political input with improved operations. To the extent that public and private actors can effectively share responsibility and ownership, great progress can be made.

Two major concerns need to be addressed for potential private sector operators and investors. First, will the local authority shareholder "interfere" in operational decisions, thereby reducing system efficiencies? Second, will the local authority use its joint shareholder and regulator power in a manner predictable enough to satisfy potential long-term investors?

Efforts to address these issues are in their very early stages. General solutions will rely on an acceptance by all parties of the need to respect other parties' objectives and roles in addressing shared problems. More project-specific solutions will have to be developed as well, however, before substantial amounts of private money will be forthcoming. New forms of regulation (possibly including

---

[27] Rivera, D., 1996: *Private Sector Participation in the Water Supply and Wastewater Sector: Lessons from Six Developing Countries*. World Bank. Washington D.C.

more parties in the regulatory body) or financial support (e.g. expanded programs for stand-by guarantees from multilateral development banks) should be explored.

A substantially different form of "joint venture" involves the NGO-led provision of water services. Instead of a for-profit operator and expensive capital investments, this approach relies on NGOs to organize the delivery of basic sanitation services, supported by public and private sector funds. One example from Addis Ababa, Ethiopia is described in Box 9.

Box 9: Addis Ababa, Ethiopia: Local, NGO-led provision of community wastewater services[28]

The sewerage system in Addis Ababa serves only 200,000 people; another 175,000 use septic tanks. 1.5 million residents share dry pit latrines and 700,000 have no access to any kind of facility at all. The municipal government has not been able to service the existing sanitation system, much less add new facilities. Neither does it have the organizational capacity to provide even small scale support for expanding the informal system.

One part of the answer has been provided by NGOs. It involves co-ordination among neighborhood "woredas," public agencies, community groups and NGOs to provide decentralized sanitation systems. Twenty-three NGOs and 19 government groups, including central municipal government and neighborhood governing councils, are implementing such projects. One third have been carried out by government entities, the other two-thirds by NGOs. Of the NGOs, eight are international groups and 15 are national organisations. The majority of government engagement comes from neighborhood councils.

In most neighborhoods, both the local-level governing body and NGOs collaborate on projects, which benefit, on average, about 5000 people. Over half of the 160 projects studied deal with stormwater drainage, a third support latrine building, and a small number address solid waste disposal. About 900 latrines are being built, serving about 100,000 people.

Forty one different donor entities, including international charities (such as CARE), foreign aid agencies and NGOs help fund the projects. NGO funding runs the gamut from international aid agencies to income generated directly from the projects.

Critical to the success of these small-scale, decentralized partnerships is government institutions, community organizations, and, most importantly, ad-hoc neighborhood committees formed in connection with the projects themselves.

Lessons

The model of civic not-for-profit private sector participation in environmental infrastructure development is long-standing and has had far-reaching effects over the years. This is particularly the case in the lowest income countries given their difficulties in attracting private investment because of

---

[28]   Alfonsi, A., 1997: "Ethiopia Urban Sanitation Support Project. Executive Summary: Addis Ababa
        Sanitation Case Study". Presented at the Conference "Business and Municipality: New Partnerships for
        the 21st Century", Bremen, Germany, March 1997.

market, credit and political risks. For many of these countries, economic globalisation is a strictly theoretical idea, and they remain, for the most part, dependent on official forms of aid for development finance.

The model has many limitations. For example, once the facilities are built, responsibility for maintenance is unclear. In addition, at least in Addis Ababa, there is a tendency for community organizing to be overzealous in engaging citizens and creating new groups, at the expense of making use of existing associations. There remains a strong need for actors and institutions capable of building on this work to establish long-term incentives for maintaining the new infrastructure.

Finally, the potential for foreign direct investors or international suppliers to contribute to such initiatives needs further exploration. Both "groups" have substantial financial and technical resources. They also have commercial, and sometimes contractual, incentives to "do good" in local markets. In some cases this is designed to build local markets, in others it is to help reduce the political risks associated with local operations. Further co-ordination of these efforts with the social development agendas of local NGOs and other organizations may help increase substantially the resources available.

Public Financial Support: Loans, Equity, Insurance, Grants

Finally, and while it does not fit the historical progression, it should be noted that even where a service is fully supplied by the private sector and substantial private investment is involved, governments may continue to provide financial support. This has taken a variety of forms in the cases described above, including: (a) loans to the company or project (as was done in the Argentina and Malaysia concessions); (b) passive shareholdings in the company (as was provided by the International Finance Corporation for Aguas Argentinas); (c) insurance for "political" and other risks (such as the political risk cover provided by the World Bank Group through MIGA); as well as (d) grants for portions of the project costs (such those used in Ethiopia or provided under UNDP's program of technical assistance for public-private partnerships in the urban sector)[28].

6.0 Conditions for Success

While a large variety of public-private partnerships are evolving, and each needs to be tailored to the local context, most of the success stories share several general conditions. They include the need for:

- **A widely-recognized crisis:** Missing or under-performing services and wasted resources fundamentally impair the ability of public and private parties to fulfill their priority objectives, and are widely recognized as such. These factors help build interest in public-private co-operation.

- **Champions:** Even if the crisis is clear and the interest is there, public-private partnerships rarely succeed without the drive and commitment of a few individuals to make it happen. They may be in government, they may be in NGOs. If one can be found among the users

---

[28]   For further information on the Yale/UNDP Program, visit its web site at http://www.undp.org/undp/ppp

they can be the best as their key goal is the provision of effective and efficient services. Regulators can also provide champions, but their role should be focused on optimizing the needs of the users and the providers. While providers have clear commercial incentives to bring partnerships together, someone else needs to make sure that the nature and price of the service they want to provide fits the local context.

- **Acceptance:** Champions cannot build a partnership alone. Others need to recognize that their individual needs can also be met through involvement in the partnership process, but only if they recognize and respect the needs of the other parties as well. Public sector workers can be a source of major opposition to increased private involvement in the provision of services. Governments may have difficulty accepting the profit motive of private businesses. Companies may walk away from the lengthy, uncertain decision-making processes often found in the public sector. Focusing on the broader, shared goals to be achieved is the only way through.

- **Credibility and transparency:** Effective co-operation among governments, businesses, NGOs and others is always difficult to achieve. It is made even more difficult if a wide range of participants are involved and there is not a high level of trust, or at least predictability, in the process. If people think there are "funny things" going on, many will be unwilling to invest their time or resources. The credibility of the champions and other leaders involved, as well as the transparency of the process used, are critical determinants of long-term success.

- **Flexibility:** Public-private partnerships are context based. They vary in target, form, process and parties. Flexibility is key. It needs to be present in the choice of parties to play the different roles, which varies from case to case. It needs to be present in the choice of response in order to maximize effectiveness and optimize system efficiency. The most successful co-operative arrangements stem from a flexible, opportunistic approach, drawing from and adapting experiences of other cases.

- **Time:** Partnerships take time. It takes time to understand the problems to be addressed, the impact on potential partners, as well as their needs and work methods. It also takes time to design responses that meet the needs of the major players, earn their respect and involvement, and provide the services. Progress can certainly be made along the way, contracts can be signed, facilities built. But the process of achieving and maintaining acceptance among users, providers and regulators is a continuing one based on co-operative dialogue to address shared needs.

7.0   Summary and Conclusions

Many critics of "public-private partnerships" view them as warm and fuzzy, but ultimately ineffective, i.e. efforts to make governments and businesses feel better about themselves. Some initiatives do fall within this characterisation. Others maintain that governments and businesses do their jobs best when they keep apart and focus on their core roles: governments setting frameworks within which markets can function and businesses thrive. There is some truth in that position as well.

But where critical problems -- such as a lack of clean water -- prevent both the public and private sectors from achieving their key goals, co-operation may be the best way to optimize the allocation of public and private resources to promote an effective resolution. Co-operation can take many forms. It may be as simple as an on-going dialogue which provides a basis for co-ordinated, but separate, efforts to address the problem. It may be as complex as a joint venture to provide long-term water services to millions of people.

The term "public-private partnerships" encompasses a wide spectrum of co-operative relationships aimed at two major targets:

- First, effectively solving problems which have a critical impact on a wide range of parties.
- Second, doing so in the most efficient manner possible by optimizing the use of public and private resources.

In these days of resource scarcity and global competitiveness, we must aim to capture any opportunities for leveraging from our individual efforts to address our shared needs. Public-private partnerships are one evolving method for doing so.

OECD PUBLICATIONS, 2, rue André-Pascal, 75775 PARIS CEDEX 16
PRINTED IN FRANCE
(97 98 05 1 P) ISBN 92-64-16083-3 – No. 50089 1998